a healing touch

Riverview Series Book 3

Melissa A. Hanson

ISBN 13: 978-0-9965485-5-7 /
ISBN 13: 978-0-9965485-8-8
EPUB: 978-0-9965485-4-0

Cover Layout & Design: Melissa A. Hanson
Image: shutterstock.com / Epic Stock Media
Editing: Christina Herrera, Founder of Romantica Publishing

Table of Contents:

Dedication:

PROLOGUE
ONE
TWO
THREE
FOUR
FIVE
SIX
SEVEN
EIGHT
NINE
TEN
ELEVEN
TWELVE
THIRTEEN
FOURTEEN
FIFTEEN
SIXTEEN
SEVENTEEN
EIGHTEEN
NINETEEN
TWENTY
TWENTY-ONE
TWENTY-TWO
TWENTY-THREE
EPILOGUE

Acknowledgements:

Resources:

About the Author:

Dedication:

Dedicated to all those special friends
that randomly come into our lives.

Who accept us for who we are.
Old and young it never matters.

Some stay in our lives longer than others,
but each will leave an imprint on us.
Forever altering our lives.

You never know how one conversation,
or one interaction may change your life or theirs.
Unless you've walked in someone's footsteps
you will never really know what they are facing on a daily basis.

A kind word, a helpful gesture
will alway brighten someone's day.
Look for the good, look for the positive,
and never be afraid to reach out a helping hand.

Reader Note:

This book includes sensitive material that may be upsetting for some readers. This book contains references to rape and suicide. I have tried to address and handle these traumatic situations in a sensitive manner.

A HEALING TOUCH

*"Healing doesn't mean the damage never existed.
It means the damage no longer controls your life."*
Akshay Dubey

PROLOGUE

~ Natasha ~

*T*he party was raging out of control. The two-story house was beyond hot and stuffy. College kids I knew, and so many that I'd never seen before, crowded the downstairs rooms where furniture had been pushed aside. Couples grinded together in the center of the room with the music blaring.

Leaving my roommate Justine as she danced in the middle of the room, I had finally found the bathroom. The line that snaked around the hall should have been the clear indicator.

Leaning against the wall I continued to search the faces of those around me looking for the one person I had hoped to see here tonight. The only reason I had even agreed to come to this party with Justine. So far it had been a bust and I was ready to go back to my dorm room. Spring quarter was coming to an end, finals were

1

only a few short weeks away, and it wouldn't be long before I would no longer be a lowly freshman.

It was my first year away from my close friends and family. I had loved the freedom being away from home and the school was beautiful. Justine had been the best roommate ever and we'd gotten along right from the start.

I pulled my long, dark, almost black, curly strands of hair off my shoulders in an attempt to cool my neck. It was useless; the narrow hallway was even more stifling hot. The line moved, but it seemed like just inches at a time.

Pulling out my phone I glanced at the time, 9 p.m. Ugh. I knew there was no way Justine was going to be ready to leave yet. This was exactly why I hadn't gone to these types of parties all year. They were just a waste of my time.

Shoving my phone back into my back pocket I glanced up and caught sight of the boy I'd had a crush on all year. Caleb Wilson. The one reason I had agreed to even come to this stupid party. His short blond hair had grown out this quarter. Even though he was looking away from me I knew his eyes were a deep brown, almost a chocolate color.

My heart started to pound and the night was quickly making a turn for the better. I had promised myself that if he showed up tonight that I was going to make an effort to talk to him, *really* talk to him this time and not just about school projects.

Caleb was a couple years older and a third-year student in the architecture program I was in. I'd been crushing on him all year. He was always friendly in the studio where all the architecture students had workspace. He often would help the first-year students answering questions and providing input on our projects.

Earlier in the week he'd casually asked if I would be coming to this party. When I just shrugged that I wasn't sure, he'd mentioned he was planning to come and that maybe he'd see me there.

Cursing the slow line, I was now anxious, wondering if maybe there was another bathroom nearby that might have a shorter line. Caleb moved further into the main room with a group of his friends. Taking count, I was now fifth in line and hoped everyone in front of me would be quick.

Finally, the last person in front of me exited the bathroom and I rushed in locking the door behind me. When I was done, I quickly washed my hands and checked my appearance in the full-length mirror that hung on the back of the door. My hair still looked decent, the bit of make-up I had put on earlier surprisingly, hadn't melted off yet. My fair skin appeared fairer due to the darkness of my hair. But the contrast made my pale blue eyes seem brighter. The simple silver hoops in my ears matched the circle silver pendant around my neck.

I had worn a white skirt tonight, which was unusual for me. I was more comfortable in jeans or leggings, but I was on a mission to step out of my comfort zone so tonight I'd opted for the skirt. It grazed about mid-thigh and was considered long by comparison to so many skirts and dresses I'd seen tonight. I could have sworn most of the girls at the party had clothing that barely covered their butt cheeks. I had rolled up the three-quarter sleeves of my red and gray plaid button down with the top of a lacy gray tank barely visible underneath.

Taking a deep breath, I left the bathroom in search of Caleb. A very drunk couple staggered into the bathroom behind me, laughing at each other. Their limbs tangled up to the point it was almost difficult to separate them.

I stepped into the main room where I'd last seen Caleb and scanned the faces, but to my huge disappointment he was nowhere to be found. I turned back to the hallway and continued to search through the rooms downstairs but couldn't find him anywhere. *Did he leave already?*

Frustrated I walked back through the kitchen. I was thirsty but there was no way I was touching the punch bowl on the counter. Who knew what was in it. Several large bottles of tequila and vodka were also scattered across the countertop. I noticed a stash of water bottles off to the side, and I figured those were probably safe. Opening the top of the water bottle, I quickly drank almost half the bottle not realizing how thirsty I really was.

Maneuvering my way through the groups of kids that were laughing and having a good time was difficult. The crowd continued to get thicker and the space between people tighter. As I re-entered the main living area the room started to spin. I tried to focus on the dancing figures around me but they all began to blur together. It was difficult to breathe, sweat broke out on my forehead as I struggled to keep the nausea down.

Where was Justine? Scanning the room, I finally found my roommate leaning against the wall talking to one of the girls that lived in our dorm. Relief flooded me as I staggered through the crowd.

Midway across the room I felt a strong arm wrap around my waist. I spun around; almost losing my balance and found myself looking up into the face of the boy I'd been searching the house for. Caleb Wilson. His deep brown eyes warmed me; a few strands of his blond hair fell into his eyes as I examined his handsome face.

"Hey, Natasha. Are you okay?"

"Hi Caleb. Um, I don't feel so well." I could barely form the words. My tongue felt like it was numb. I was so tired all of a sudden. Keeping my eyes open was difficult. I didn't feel right and I didn't know what was wrong. I felt my legs collapse under me and then I felt weightless as I was scooped up into Caleb's strong arms. I sighed as I leaned my head against his warm chest and darkness surrounded me.

CHAPTER ONE

~ *Natasha* ~

*L*ight trickled into the room through the open blinds. My limbs felt heavy and I ached everywhere. The crack of thunder in the distance startled me. Pushing myself upright to sit on the edge of the bed I was laying in, I realized I was not in my dorm room. *Where the hell was I?*

My purse was laying on the nightstand. I grabbed it and searched for my cell phone. I had several texts, missed calls, and voicemails from Justine. Panic sliced through me. My phone read 9:30 am. The last thing I remembered was being on the dance floor the night before. Almost twelve hours ago.

Standing up I straightened my twisted skirt and looked around the strange bedroom. It was sparse with only a dresser in the corner next to the window. The sky beyond was dark and full of storm clouds. The bed was rumpled, the comforter was on the floor. The only other piece of furniture was the nightstand.

I realized I was still wearing one of my ballet flats, but the other one was missing. Searching the floor, I found my missing shoe, as well as a piece of white fabric that was partially visible under the bed. I realized it was my panties.

Scared to touch them I was sure I was in a nightmare. My heart was slamming against my chest.

A HEALING TOUCH

What had been one of my favorite pair of panties were now slightly torn at the side and crumpled onto the carpet.

I thought I was going to faint, I tasted bile in the back of my throat causing it to burn. *This cannot be happening to me!* I picked them up carefully off the floor and tossed them into my purse.

I tried to push air back into my lungs and think. *Deep breathes, breath in, breathe out,* I kept telling myself as I ran through the events from the previous night. But everything was fuzzy and at the moment all I knew was that I had to get out of here–wherever here was.

Stumbling out of the room I found myself in a hallway. It was quiet and I didn't see anyone. I hurried down the hall and found a flight of stairs. Not wanting to be in this house a minute longer I raced down them.

Downstairs, there were people crashed all over the living room and I realized I was in the same house where the party had been last night. Reaching the front door, I flung it open. The smell of rain in the air tingled my nose as lighting shot through the sky followed quickly by a loud crack of thunder.

My nerves already on high alert seemed to intensify with the electricity racing through the air. The storm was going to be a strong one, the wind was already whipping through the streets.

Slamming the front door shut behind me I fumbled for my car keys as tears streaked down my face. The wind was strong as it blew my hair across my face, blinding me as I struggled to push the dark strands away.

The sinister clouds above opened up and large drops of rain began pelting me as I rushed the last few feet down the street towards where I remembered leaving my car.

Relief washed over me as I found my car exactly where I'd left it the night before. Unlocking the doors, I slid behind the wheel tossing my purse in the seat next to me. Hysteria was beginning to overtake me and my crying took on a whole new level. I was soaked and water ran down my face, the salty tears mixing with rain.

Sobbing, I bent over resting my head on the steering wheel and tried to pull myself together so that I could drive back to the dorm.

Knocking on my passenger window caused me to jump in my seat. A scream caught in my throat as I looked into the eyes of an older gentleman holding an umbrella.

"Miss, are you okay?" he asked through the glass.

"I'll be fine. I'm headed home."

"Okay, be careful the roads are slick."

"Thank you."

I could tell he was worried and I didn't need to draw any more attention to myself. I pushed the button to start the car and pulled away from the curb. I brushed more tears away as I tried to focus on the previous night. I hadn't even wanted to go to the party but Justine had begged me to go with her.

Maybe nothing really happened, maybe I just passed out. *Think positive, Natasha!* I chided myself. Clinging to that thought I continued to try to reconstruct the night. I was driving and I had only drunk the bottled water that I'd found in the kitchen. I knew better than to try the punch. *So, what happened? Why couldn't I remember going upstairs? Why had my underwear been tossed on the floor?*

By the time I reached the dorm ten minutes later I still had no answers. Justine and I had been there a couple hours when I left her to use the restroom. I remembered seeing Caleb, and then searching for him after I was done in the restroom. I know I had picked up a water bottle and then walked back into the main room to find Justine. The house had been hot with the number of kids crowded in the space. I know I had been drinking the water as I walked back toward Justine. I remember feeling flushed, overheated, and dizzy.

I think I ran into Caleb and I said hi, but I couldn't be sure. But then I had this memory of being carried, and held against a strong chest, but again I'm not sure. Everything beyond that and when I woke up this morning was blank. Like it had never happened. I finally reached my room and when I opened the door, I found Justine pacing the floor.

"Oh my God! I've been so worried about you! Where the hell have you been?" She flung herself at me giving me a big hug and then almost immediately pulling back to look at me closer. "What's wrong? What happened to you? You've got mascara streaked all the way down your face."

"I don't know. I woke up this morning upstairs in the house where the party was. I don't know how I got there and a good chunk of the night is missing."

"WHAT? Come, sit down." Justine pulled me to my bed, sitting next to me. "I've been texting and calling you all night. Caleb said you weren't feeling well and that he was going to bring you back to the dorm. I told him I'd come with him that I wanted to make sure you were okay, but he insisted you were fine and that you said I should stay. I knew you'd had a crush on him all year so I was all excited for you thinking maybe it would give you time together. I didn't stay too much longer. Carol was coming back to the dorm and I caught a ride with her. Then when I got here and you weren't here and I started to worry."

"I don't know. I don't remember that. I vaguely remember sweating, and getting dizzy. I think I remember Caleb, but it's fuzzy I can't be sure. Then I woke up by myself in a bedroom upstairs."

"Do you think anything happened?" Justine's voice was low and concerned as her hand reached over to my knee.

"I don't know Justine. I really don't know. I'm scared. I found my panties on the floor." It was hard for me to get the last few words out. Tears began to slip down my cheek as I watched my friend and roommate.

"Oh, Natasha." She sighed as she pulled me into a hug. I sagged against her, resting my head on her shoulder.

"What if something did happen Justine?" I whispered my biggest fear. I pulled back a bit, wiping the tears away.

Justine reached around me to the Kleenex box that sat on a small table next to the head of my bed. "Here. Do you have any marks, or bruises? Does it feel like you've had sex?"

"I haven't really looked. My whole body aches. I just feel weird, off. It's hard to explain."

"You need to look. Don't pee if you can help it. Natasha, if something did happen last night you need to go to the hospital and get checked out."

"I can't believe this is happening. It's not real. It can't be." I brushed away more tears as they slipped down my cheeks.

"Go in the bathroom and look. If you need me for anything just yell. I think no matter what though you should go get checked. If something did happen, the sooner you go, the better the chance they'll be able to collect any evidence that might be useful."

"I just want to take a hot shower and forget about the whole thing."

"I know love, but you have to do this. I'm right here for you. Go, the longer we wait the harder it's going to be."

I stood up and walked to our attached bathroom. Shutting the door behind me I leaned against it trying to gather my courage and strength. Looking in the mirror, it was almost as if a stranger stared back at me.

My long, wavy, almost black hair was slightly tangled. My usually bright blue eyes seemed dull. As Justine had said, I had mascara streaks all the way down my cheeks. I grabbed a washcloth, wetted it and rubbed my cheeks cleaning off the black marks. I examined my face for any other scratches or marks, then my arms, nothing. I lifted up my shirt. My stomach appeared okay. My bra was shifted though. My heart sank and tears pooled once again.

My left breast had a large reddish-purple bruise. Carefully, I lifted my skirt to check my legs and thighs and stifled a sob as I slid to the floor. I had dried blood smeared on the upper inner thigh. I sat propped against the wall, hugging my knees to my chest, my head resting on my knees and cried. The door creaked open.

"Oh no." Justine sighed as she sat next to me, her arm around me. "Natasha, come on we need to get you to the hospital."

Shaking my head no, I sat there on the cold floor. The coldness seeping into my bones. I felt humiliated. I just wanted to forget it all, wipe it all away.

"I know you don't want to do this, but you have to document it. Otherwise there's no way to prove anything."

"Justine, do you think Caleb did this?" I looked up at her.

"I don't know love. I would hope not. Come on, you have to get up."

Justine pulled me up, hugging me tight to her. I had no strength left and I leaned against her. I knew she was right. I needed to get to the hospital, but once I did then it would be real. I didn't want it to be real.

Numbness enveloped me. I could feel myself quickly becoming desensitized by everything around me. Retreating somewhere deep inside myself. Somewhere I'd never been before. Picking up my purse, I handed my keys to Justine as I felt a fog descend around me.

The short ride to the hospital was quiet. The rain had slowed to a light trickle, but the storm wasn't done yet. The clouds were still dark and ominous. It was fitting, gloomy weather for a bleak day.

Staring out the window the lush green trees and landscape passed by in a blur. The constant rain and green of Oregon were a stark contrast to my hometown in Southern California. I had loved the city I now lived in and the school on first sight. Having a full scholarship had sweetened the deal, even though I'd left my two best friends Bailey and Mia. The three of us had been inseparable during the last couple of years in high school.

I looked over at Justine as she drove through the wet streets. We'd been complete strangers at the beginning of the year. It didn't take us long though to become close friends. It was like we'd known each other forever.

She was tense as she drove. It wasn't often I saw her rattled. Justine was always so calm and in control. She was studying Biology as her major with the intent to pursue a medical degree. For now, her preference was to work as an Emergency Room doctor and I knew it would probably be a good fit for her.

She turned to look at me. "You're going to be okay."

"I hope so," I whispered as I turned back to the rain slick window and wondered if anything in my life would ever be okay again.

CHAPTER TWO

~ *Natasha* ~

The emergency room at the local hospital was surprisingly empty with only a scattering of people sitting in the rows of plastic chairs. I was numb and cold. Each step I took toward the check in station was one more reminder that I wasn't having a nightmare, but that I was living one. Justine was by my side every step of the way. The receptionist at the desk looked up from her computer screen as we reached the open window.

"Can I help you?"

"Um, I ah…" I was having difficulty searching for the words. To say them out loud meant I had to acknowledge them. My brain was shutting down, refusing to cooperate.

The receptionist was older, probably older than my mom, and her hazel eyes were kind. I felt Justine's hand take my cold and clammy one in hers and squeeze it tight. I was relieved when she finally spoke the words that I wasn't able to utter.

"We were at a party last night. My friend came back to our dorm this morning with no recollection of last night. She may have been raped."

The receptionist pulled a clipboard out and handed it to me through the window. "Please fill this out and return it to me. We'll get you right in."

A HEALING TOUCH

Justine gently guided me to an empty corner. The cold plastic of the chair bit into my back as I stared at the form in front of me. I tried to focus on answering the basic questions: name, address, age, lists to check yes and no. I finally reached the end, scribbled my name and returned the clipboard.

It wasn't long before the double doors leading further into the hospital opened and my name was called. I reached for Justine and tugged her along with me. I knew this was going to be tough enough. I was scared and I didn't want to be alone. I had no idea what to expect or how long this was going to take.

We followed the petite nurse down several halls until she reached a room and motioned us in. My senses were on high alert. Everything around me was more intense. The smell of cleaning products, alcohol wipes, the smell of unclean bodies, and sickness all intermingling. It was all I could do to keep myself from turning around and escaping this nightmare.

"My name is Katie. Go ahead and have a seat on the exam table. Are you in any immediate pain or injury?"

I sat at the edge of the table, the paper crinkling under me, my feet slightly dangling from the edge. "No."

"Okay. I'm going to be here with you every step. I'm sorry but this will probably be difficult and it takes some time. We have a woman doctor on call today. She'll be in shortly and we'll walk you through the process. You are welcome to have your friend stay here with you. I'll be right back."

The nurse left, the door shutting behind her. I looked around the small, windowless exam room. It was sterile and I felt dirty, more so as I sat on the table and waited.

My heart began beating faster, the unknown of what was ahead dark and overwhelming. Justine had taken a seat in the corner.

"Natasha, you're doing the right thing."

I looked over at my friend. Her dark blonde hair was pulled back into a ponytail. Her brown eyes searched mine. "I know, but I'm scared Justine." Tears pooled behind my eyelids and threatened to break loose at any moment. My hands gripped the side of the table, my knuckles white.

A knock on the door startled me. An older woman with her gray hair held on top of her head with a clip stepped inside the room. Katie, the nurse that had escorted us to the room was directly behind her.

"Hi Natasha, I'm Dr. Randall. My nurse will be here with me through the entire process. Before we get started though I need to ask you a few questions."

"Okay."

"Have you called the police or filed a police report?"

"No. Do I need to?"

"You don't need to right now. You can decide that later. The most important thing is that you are here now. The more time that passes, the harder it is to collect the valuable evidence. Would you like me to call the local Sexual Assault Crisis Center? They can have a staff member help you through this process and help you after."

"No, I'm okay right now. My friend Justine, will stay here with me."

"Okay. I'm going to explain the entire process, step by step. At any time, if you have questions, or feel uncomfortable, or want me to stop, all you have to do is say so. We'll try to make this as painless as possible. First can you tell me what happened?"

I repeated the same information that I'd given Justine. The doctor typed notes into the computer as she sat on the small stool that rolled around on the floor. Katie stood at the counter and I watched as she was pulling out bags, instruments, a comb, slides, and several other items on a tray. Hearing my name repeated a couple of times snapped my attention back to Dr. Randall.

"Huh? Sorry what was that?" I asked.

"I asked if you've had any consensual sex in the past few days?"

"No, I've never been with anyone before." I read the sympathy in her face and for some reason it just made the injury worse. To know I'd never be able to offer my virginity to someone special. I'd waited to find a special person and in the end my choice was taken from me, no longer mine to freely give.

I sat on the table and felt like I was no longer in my body. Like I had somehow separated myself and was viewing from afar.

"Have you gone to the bathroom, showered, or changed clothes?"

"No."

"Okay, that's a good thing. Let's get started."

Several hours later, I was curled up on the hospital bed. I pulled the hospital gown tighter; my knees were drawn up almost to my chest. I couldn't hold back the tears and they continued to stream down the side of my face.

Somehow, I'd managed through the examination, the samples, the collection of my clothing, the multitude of handouts with information on rape counseling, sexual transmitted diseases, and my rights without completely losing it. But now that I was alone, I couldn't hold back any longer.

Justine would be back soon with a change of clothes for me, since all of the clothing I'd been wearing was now bundled up in bags with identification tags.

The only good thing, was that it looked like a condom had been used. So, while my chances of getting pregnant or a sexual transmitted disease was reduced, it meant there was less evidence in the event I decided to try to prosecute.

I wasn't sure I wanted to go to the police or file a report. What was the point? I had no idea who might have done it. I had no memories of it. I just wanted to bury it and forget it ever happened.

By the time we were back at the dorm it was late Sunday afternoon. I headed straight for the shower. Stripping off the sweats and tennis shoes that Justine had brought me I stood underneath the scalding hot water as it washed over my body. Taking the soap, I scrubbed everything until my skin was almost red.

The bruising on my left breast was darker than it had been this morning and it was a reminder that something had happened the previous night.

Tears fell as the steam from the hot water swallowed up the entire bathroom. I wasn't sure how long I'd been standing under the water, but I couldn't stand any longer. I sank to the floor of the shower and sat, hugging my knees and cried until the water turned cold.

I finally shut the water off, pulled myself out of the shower and dried off.

I wiped the mirror and stared at my reflection. My features looked the same, except my eyes were red and puffy from crying. But I felt like I wasn't looking at myself anymore.

Wrapping myself in my fluffy aqua bathrobe I left the bathroom. Justine had been lying on her bed reading a book, but quickly sat up setting it aside as I made my way over to my bed.

"I can go pick us up some food. Whatever you'd like."

"I'm not really hungry," I replied as I sat on the edge of my bed.

"You need to eat something. You haven't had anything all day."

"You pick then, I don't know what I want." I pulled the covers back and slid between my sheets.

Justine walked over and sat next to me. Her hand rested on my arm. "I'm here for you love. Whatever you need, you just say it. No matter what time of the day or night. Okay?"

"Thanks Justine, it means a lot. It really does. I'm tired. I think I'm going to try to take a nap."

"Okay. I'll go find us something to eat and I'll be back soon. If you're sleeping do you want me to just let you be or do you want me to wake you?"

"If you bring hot food wake me. If it's cold food just let me sleep."

"You got it."

I laid there in my bed as the door to our room closed. My blankets pulled up to my chin. I was exhausted. My skin was raw from scrubbing it, and I tried to ignore the ache between my legs that was a reminder of what I'd lost. Knowing there was no way I'd ever get it back again.

I didn't think it was possible for me to shed anymore tears. But I was wrong as my eyes welled up and the moisture slid down the side of my face. Wiping them away I shut my eyes. Thankfully, I slipped into a dreamless sleep.

CHAPTER THREE

~ *Natasha* ~

Justine was shaking me awake. I knew it was her, but the touch on my arm caused my heart to beat faster. My breathing was rapid as I gasped for breath. I slowly opened my eyes, trying not to rip my arm from her touch. My skin crawled and I hated the reaction I had to a simple touch on my arm.

"Hey there, you screamed out in your sleep. Scared the crap out of me. Are you okay?"

Was I okay? What a loaded question. No, I didn't think I was, but I didn't want to worry her further. "Sorry, yeah I'm okay."

Justine sat on the side of my bed; her face full of worry. She was like an open book. I always knew where I stood with her and what she was thinking. It was written all over her face. "Are you sure you don't want to go to one of the therapists on the list they gave you? It might help."

"Maybe later. I don't want to think about it right now, okay?" I could hear the bite in my words as they came out harsher than I had intended. I knew she only was trying to help. I had finals in a week and I needed to push this all aside and focus on those right now. Maybe if I didn't think about it, I could forget this whole weekend had ever happened.

"Yeah, okay. I'm sorry. I'm just worried about you."

"I didn't mean to snap at you. I know you're only trying to help." I reached for my phone and realized it was still early. "I'm going to sleep a bit longer okay?"

"Sure. I'll be quiet getting ready."

I rolled over and faced the wall. Justine's first class started before mine. I still had a couple hours before I'd need to get up and get ready. Staring at the beige concrete block wall, I willed my brain to quit thinking and let myself go back to sleep. I could hear Justine in our bathroom as she got ready. Finally, my eyes drifted shut.

Waking to the screeching of my alarm, I rolled over to reset it. I needed just a bit longer before I had to face the outside world. The room was quiet. My bed was warm as I pulled the blankets tighter around me. I was chilled, but from the inside out, if that was even possible. I felt disconnected to my body and I didn't know how to find "me" again.

Maybe having no memories of the entire night was a blessing in disguise since I wouldn't have to relive the event over and over again in my head. But I felt like my body remembered in some odd fashion, like it knew what had happened, and I didn't know if that was a good or bad thing. I groaned when my alarm went off once again. I knew I needed to get moving or I'd be late for class.

A HEALING TOUCH

Thankfully my day was uneventful. I moved from class to class almost in a trancelike state. I hated how jumpy I was around people. Walking into the architecture studio I slid into my chair. I'd planned to work the rest of the evening on my final project for the quarter. I had a lot to do and I was quickly running out of time.

Pulling out my laptop I began setting it up. I shifted a stack of trace paper of my current design revisions to make room for my computer. Buried under the stack of paper I noticed an envelope with only my name printed on the front. I looked around the room but no one seemed to be watching me. Sliding the piece of paper out of the envelope I read the simple words.

> I had a fun time with you the other night. Knowing I was your first made it even better. Can't wait to be with you again. I hope you enjoyed it as much as I did.

My heart dropped and I thought I was going to be sick to my stomach. Tears threatened and I tried to pull myself together. My hands were shaking and my brain went numb. I quickly crumpled up the note wanting to throw it in the trash, but not sure if I should. A hand on my shoulder made me jump. A scream almost escaped from my lips.

"Woah, sorry, didn't mean to scare you. Are you okay?"

I turned and found myself looking up at Caleb's handsome face, his deep brown eyes searching mine. I'm not sure if I felt relief or if I was a bit frightened. I was so confused. Deep down I didn't think Caleb could be the one, but how could I be sure?

"No, not really. Caleb, can I ask you something?" my voice was so quiet–the words slow and deliberate–like my brain had to think about formulating each one as I put the sentence together.

"Sure, you know I'm always here to help."

"Saturday night. What happened?" I searched his face looking for any sign of regret or guilt but his expression gave away nothing.

"What do you mean what happened? Are you talking about when you practically passed out in my arms? You didn't look well. I told you that I'd take you back to your dorm. When we got outside, you refused to come with me, and you demanded that I put you down. You sat on the front steps, and told me you were going to sit there and get some fresh air while you waited for Justine. I asked you several times if you were sure. But you told me you were fine. That you just wanted to wait for Justine."

His story lined up with what he'd told Justine. He didn't seem to hesitate at all in his story. I wanted to believe him. I really did, but how could I know for sure? "That's it?"

"That's it. Before I finally left, I asked you one more time if you wanted me to take you to your dorm and you waved me off, so I left."

"Did you see anyone else talk to me? Or approach me?"

"No, I left. Why? What happened Natasha?"

I shook my head. There was no way I was going to say anything to him. "Nothing. Never mind."

"You don't look so good. Are you sure there isn't anything I can do?"

"No, I'm fine. Really."

"Okay, well I'm here if you need anything. How's your project coming along? Did you get those changes incorporated that we worked on last week?"

"Not yet. I was going to work on them this evening. Thanks again for all your help this quarter. I know you have your own work to finish."

"It's no problem. You've got a special talent. Your designs are clean and simple, but you have an amazing way of pulling all the little details together that make your projects stand out. I only wish I had a fraction of your natural ability."

"You're crazy. Your projects are the best every time you present. I only hope I can be as successful." My stomach was starting to settle a bit as we moved on to more neutral topics.

The note I still held crumpled in my hand was proof that something had happened Saturday night and there was someone out there that knew what it was. But did I really want to know what had happened? I was torn. Part of me just wanted to bury it all and forget the night ever happened. Really, what would I gain by trying to find the answers? More pain?

"Well, I'll be working most of the evening. My presentation is first in our group this time, so I've got a lot to finish up. Let me know if you need any help though."

I looked up at Caleb, his chiseled cheeks indented slightly. His short blond hair tousled like he'd been out in the wind. He always seemed carefree and lighthearted whenever he was around, and had always been so kind to me all year. Could I have been such a bad judge of character? I sure hoped not.

I tried to plaster a slight smile on my face. "Thanks Caleb, you've really been a big help and I can't tell you how much I appreciate it." I could hear the waver in my voice as I struggled to hold back the emotions that I was so desperate to ignore and bury.

Immediately, I could see concern in Caleb's deep brown eyes, and I wanted to kick myself. I was failing miserably at hiding my feelings. I felt Caleb's strong fingertips on my shoulder as my entire body stiffened.

"Natasha, are you really okay? I've never seen you like this."

I held my shoulders in place even though every bone in my body wanted to shrug off his hand from my shoulder. His touch left a burning sensation that radiated from my shoulder down my body, making my skin crawl. "I'm just tired, I didn't sleep enough this weekend and I have a lot to finish."

"I understand, but you have to try to take it easy or you're going to burn yourself out. This program is intense and you have four more years to go."

"Thanks Caleb. I'm fine, really."

"Okay. If you need anything, let me know."

I watched him finally walk away. The breath I'd been holding in released as a sigh, and my hands shook as a chill ran down my spine. I leaned my head onto my arms and tried to pull myself together.

I still held the crumpled note in my hand. It felt like it was burning through my flesh. I kept telling myself quietly *one breath at a time, just take one breath at a time.* Finally, getting myself somewhat under control I shoved the crumpled note in my bag and finished setting up my laptop.

Staring at the screen in front of me I tried to make the changes to my floor plan. My sketches on the desk blurred. I felt completely disconnected as I moved the walls around, shifting doors and windows in the computer program, almost automatically. My back was stiff from sitting in my chair, my neck ached and I was so behind. I struggled to keep my mind focused on the screen when all that kept running through my head were the words on the note I had found.

Knowing someone might be watching me at any moment and not knowing who it might be was terrifying. Completely and utterly terrifying. Finally, I couldn't take it anymore. I needed to be in my own dorm room. I couldn't work here in the open. Completely exposed. I saved my file and shut my laptop. Gathering up my sketches I tossed them in my laptop bag and I rushed out of the studio.

The cool air outside helped calm me slightly as I walked quickly back to my dorm room. My backpack and laptop bag were heavy on my back almost symbolic of the burden I felt weighing down on me. I wished I could turn back time and had just stayed in the dorm Saturday night instead of going to that stupid party.

I finally reached my dorm and maneuvered quickly through the halls to my room. Unlocking the door I hurried inside, shutting the door behind me, and only after the door was locked did I feel a sense of relief wash over me.

The room was empty. Justine was probably still in the library studying. She rarely came back to the dorm until late, especially with finals around the corner. I shrugged off my backpack and placed my laptop bag on my bed. I still felt dirty. No matter how hard I scrubbed my skin, or how hot I let the water run, it was like I couldn't get rid of the feeling. Grabbing a clean pair of leggings and an oversized t-shirt I went to the bathroom to take another hot shower, hoping that maybe it would help me relax.

I was propped up on my bed, with my laptop. It was already pushing into the early morning hours, but that was typical for me. I'd had to adapt right away to the late hours. The first couple of weeks of school had been a struggle as I got adjusted to the lack of sleep. The architecture program wasn't easy. It was intense, very time consuming and I'd learn to function on less sleep. Overnighters became the norm.

The Bachelor of Architecture degree that I was working on was a five-year program, so I knew the next four years were going to be more of the same. The sooner I adjusted the better. I flipped through the different plans that I'd put together. Surprisingly, I was happy with the progress I'd made on my project since leaving the studio.

Justine had come back several hours ago and was already asleep. I knew she had been surprised to find me in the dorm when she returned. I usually spent the evenings in the studio where I could get input, and typically I enjoyed having my classmates around me. But now I found solace in the silence.

Justine never questioned anything. She even went back out to grab me some dinner when she realized I hadn't eaten anything. She was a great friend and I didn't know what I would do without her. I couldn't bring myself to tell her about the note though. I was still pretty shaken by it.

Realizing that it was close to three a.m. I finally decided to call it quits. I opened up my calendar for the next day to see if I had anything important due. I started to panic, realizing I'd totally forgotten about the internship interview that I'd scheduled in the afternoon with one of the most respected architecture firms in the area: DeLuca Architects. I hadn't planned on even interviewing for any local internships this summer, since I thought I'd go home to Riverview and find a job there.

One of my professors knew about the opening and he persuaded me to at least go to the interview. If it didn't work out, then I hadn't lost anything.

I had done my research and I knew the company was family run, with three generations of DeLuca's currently working in the firm. Part of me was excited for the opportunity, and the other part wanted to go home for the summer. At this point, I wasn't sure which I was hoping for more.

Shutting down my computer, I crawled under the warm covers, pulling them tightly around me. It wasn't long before I surrendered to my exhaustion.

CHAPTER FOUR

~ *Natasha* ~

Pushing through the double frameless glass doors of the single-story building, I admired my surroundings. The design was modern, yet it didn't feel stark or sterile like so many modern buildings and design. There was a homeyness to it, but it was mainly in the subtle details.

My boots echoed on the polished concrete floor as I approached the reception desk where an older lady sat. She looked to be around my mom's age. Her deep brown eyes looked up and her smile was genuine. I was immediately at ease and the knots in my stomach slowly began to lessen.

"Hi, I'm Natasha Wakefield. I have an interview for the summer internship."

"Welcome Natasha, please have a seat. I'm Camille DeLuca. My husband, Thomas will be with you shortly."

"Thank you." Carrying my laptop bag, I sat down in one of the adjacent white womb chairs. There was a cluster of three nestled around a small low round table. I had to lean all the way back and I immediately felt like I was in a recliner. I could easily have closed my eyes and fallen asleep it was so comfortable.

My eyes searched the details of my surroundings, noting the neutral colors on the walls, the indirect lighting that accented construction project photos hanging on the wall opposite of where I sat. A large opening to the side of the reception desk allowed a glimpse into an open work area with a handful of desks, a few were empty, but I could also see employees with headphones focused on their screens.

DeLuca Architects was a smaller firm and I knew in a smaller firm I'd be more likely to learn a wider variety of tasks instead of having to do more repetitive tasks in a larger office. The white and chrome clock on the wall across from me clicked away the minutes.

The phone rang on Camille's desk. Simultaneously, a tall, dark haired guy walked through the open office area. His white button-down shirt was slightly open at the neck, his sleeves rolled, his dark charcoal pants were perfectly creased. He stopped at a desk and leaned over as he gestured to the screen talking with the employee. He looked a little older than me, but not by a lot. He finished talking to the employee, straightened and when he looked up, he caught me watching him. From the distance, I couldn't tell what color his eyes were, but I felt his intensity. I broke contact, looking down at my hands resting on my bag. I had been caught staring and I could already feel my cheeks burning. A dead give away on how embarrassed I was.

I noticed movement at Camille's desk and it sounded like she was finishing her call. Looking toward the reception desk I realized the guy was now standing at the desk, his attention was focused towards Camille though. Now that he was closer, I could see his features a bit better. He had a dark stubble across his cheeks, his jaw was defined. A slightly square chin. His short dark hair was thick, and full eyebrows that defined his eyes. He was ruggedly handsome, but yet still boyish.

"Troy, honey, can you take Natasha back to the conference room? She has an appointment with your dad."

Troy turned slightly his eyes catching mine. I felt like he could see though me. I didn't like how unsettled I was now. My heart was pounding, and part of me just wanted to run. I hated the fear and uncertainty that now seemed to be forever present. I wondered if it would ever go away. I took a deep breath and tried to calm my nerves.

Leaning forward, I extracted myself from the warmth and comfort of the chair I'd been sitting in. I shoved my panic and fear aside, trying to bury it so deep within me that it would never surface. It was much easier to ignore than to deal.

"Sure, Mom. Natasha, follow me please."

Following behind Troy, my footsteps echoed on the concrete floor until I reached the carpet at the edge of the open work area. Troy looked over his shoulder to make sure I was following. He stopped until I reached him.

"So, what brings you to DeLuca Architects today?

His voice was deep, calming, and confident. Everything I wasn't right at this moment.

"I have an interview for the summer internship." I almost didn't even recognize my own voice. It was so soft and almost squeaky. I was never going to get this position. I wasn't even sure why I was wasting my time.

Troy never faltered as he continued to guide me through the office. "Well good luck. We've got some really great projects in the works right now. This summer is going to be a busy one. Here you go. Just have a seat. My dad will be in shortly."

A HEALING TOUCH

I walked into the large conference room. The glass wall allowed visibility to the entire open office. The large panes of glass were butted together with no frames. The lights in the conference room popped on as soon as I stepped through the door. I took a seat in one of the gray chairs that were nestled around the large table. The chair I sat in gave me visibility out into the open office space. I watched Troy walk across the large area, enter a glass enclosed office and sat behind a desk. His attention quickly focused on the computer monitor in front of him. Setting my laptop bag on the table, I pulled out my computer and started it up.

As my computer ran through its startup process, I watched the small group in the open area in front of me work. The atmosphere was comfortable, relaxed, but professional. The longer I sat there the more I felt the pull, the desire to make a good impression, to do what it took to land this internship for the summer. Previous doubt that I had earlier was stomped to the ground and I felt a bit of my old self beginning to peak back out.

I didn't want to go home for the summer. It was safer to stay away from my friends and family right now and this was my out. I missed them, but I also didn't want them to know about what had happened. I knew if they saw me they'd read me like an open book, knowing something was up. I needed time to work through things before I went home.

Tapping the keyboard, I quickly brought up some of my favorite projects and examples of my work.

"Welcome Natasha. I'm Thomas DeLuca."

The deep voice from the doorway startled me as I had been so focused on my computer screen; I hadn't seen the older gentleman enter the room. I quickly stood, pushing back my chair, and reaching across the table to shake the hand that was offered.

"Thank you for taking the time to see me. I'm excited to see what your firm has to offer for the summer internship." I was relieved that my voice was solid and not wavering. I could do this. I knew I could. I just had to stay focused on my work. I kept the mantra in my head.

I could see where Troy got his features from. He was almost a spitting image of his father. Just a younger version. Thomas had gray sprinkled through his short dark hair, the stubble on his face was a mix of gray and dark. His eyes were light in color, from this distance it was hard to tell if they were pale blue or gray.

"Please sit."

Thomas sat in the adjacent chair at the head of the table, placing a note pad and pen on the table in front of him. I repositioned myself in the chair and prepared myself as best I could.

"Let me give you a bit of background on DeLuca Architects. As you have noticed we're a pretty small firm. Many of our employees started working here as interns and have stayed on. The company was started by my father, Nicolas. He still has his office here though he doesn't come in much anymore. To be honest, I actually think he just comes in to get away from my mother." He chuckled. "Most of our family has worked here in some shape or form over the years. Not everyone stayed in the field but many of us did. You met my wife Camille. She takes care of the books and basically runs the office. Shhh...don't tell her I admitted that."

I watched the smile spread across his face. It was clear he admired her and the love was obvious. I began to relax even more as I listened to him.

A HEALING TOUCH

"Troy is our son, He's one of the project managers and is in the process of finishing up his architectural licensing exams. Jordan is our other Licensed Architect. He's been with the company just over ten years. We also have four designers, slash draftspeople who work with myself, and both Troy and Jordan.

Workloads shift and are assigned, depending on what projects we are working on and what the deadlines are. Everyone does a little bit of everything around here. Because we're a small firm it will give you a lot of experience in different areas. We're pretty laid back and casual, but we also work hard. Sometimes evening and weekend work is needed to meet deadlines. Some projects are on a shorter schedule and more hectic. Others, we have a more relaxed time frame.

We understand that as an intern there's a lot to learn, but we also don't babysit. We're looking for someone who can take an initiative and run with it. Be given a task and after instruction can complete it. At the end of our internships, we do an evaluation and most of our interns are offered a permanent position with our firm.

Our projects range from large commercial projects, custom residential projects, to small remodeling projects. So now that you have a bit of information about who we are and what we do, tell me a little bit about yourself and why you think you might be a good fit here at DeLuca."

"I'm finishing my first year, I've maintained all A's in all my core architectural and studio classes. I've enjoyed the challenge this year. I got interested in the architectural field when I was in high school, but it wasn't until my first few classes this year that I realized how much.

Architecture is about design but I also enjoy the more practical side. I like taking a puzzle and putting it together, that's basically what any project starts out as. A bunch of puzzle pieces and the requirement is to find the solution. When it all falls into place it becomes whole.

Seeing a finished product is the best feeling. Knowing that you've created something and once it's built you've been a part of something that is going to make an impact, a lingering impression on the world and those that occupy the space.

I'd like to find a smaller firm to work in, like yours so that I'd have the opportunity to work on a variety of things. I like the more close-knit feeling of a smaller firm instead of feeling like an ant in a large firm."

"Are you from around here?"

"No, I'm from Southern California. Born and grew up there. My family is there."

"There's some really great architectural schools in Southern California. What brought you to Oregon?"

"I wanted a change. I love the green here, the smaller community. I do love where I grew up, but ultimately, I wanted to see and try something different. I'm also not so far away that I can't go home to visit with a quick flight. It was hard though to leave my friends and family, but I think it's also given me a chance to grow."

"Do you have some examples of your work you can share?"

"Yes, of course." I quickly finished pulling up my digital portfolio that displayed the work I'd completed during the year and then pushed my laptop closer to Thomas. He slid my computer closer to him and all I could do was wait while he flipped through the work.

His face and expressions were unreadable. I had no way of telling if he liked what he saw or if he wasn't impressed. My instructors had always given me really good feedback, but that was school and in class. This was the real world, and completely different.

After a few short minutes he slid my laptop back to me. "Very nice work Natasha. Especially for a first-year student. Your quality of work is obvious. You should be proud. We do have two other applicants to interview this week and then I'll let you know what our decision is. Thank you so much for taking the time to come in today and for your interest in our firm."

"Thank you very much for the opportunity. I look forward to hearing from you soon. I made a copy of my resume and projects. It's all here on this thumb drive."

Reaching across the table I set the thumb drive down as Thomas pushed back his chair. He picked up the drive while gathering his notebook and pen. Looking down I realized that he hadn't made any notes and my heart sank. There was probably no way I got the job. I tried to push back my immediate disappointment as I stood up and plastered a smile on my face as I shook his hand.

"Take your time. Camille will see you out. Thank you again, and best of luck."

Thomas then left the conference room and vanished. I slumped in my chair and sighed. I turned my attention back to my laptop as I quickly closed my files and shut it down. I slid it back into my bag and quickly walked out of the room toward the reception area. Heat flooded my face once again and I felt like I was being watched. I looked over my shoulder at the open work area, but everyone seemed to be engrossed in their computer screens. Turning around, I just wanted to escape. If this didn't pan out, I would probably be going home for the summer and I needed to start to prepare myself for that.

Camille's smiling face met me when I entered the reception area. "It was good to meet you Natasha. Thanks for coming in."

"Thank you." I smiled back and quickly pushed through the double glass doors I'd entered less than thirty minutes before.

~ *Troy* ~

Staring at my computer I tried to focus on the screen in front of me, but I couldn't keep myself from glancing at Natasha as she sat in the conference room. She wore her dark, almost jet-black hair down, her blue eyes startling bright in comparison. The casual dress she wore hugged her curves, but wasn't overly tight. She looked and appeared comfortable. There was something so familiar about her, but I couldn't put my finger on what it was. The more I watched her, the more I sensed it. But whatever it was, stayed just out of my grasp.

I pulled up the profile information about her and glanced through her basic information that she had filled out on the internship application, but nothing there triggered any additional memories. She wasn't from around here, and had only lived in Oregon since fall when school started, so I knew we hadn't run into each other before then.

Movement in the conference room drew my attention and I realized my dad had joined her and begun the interview. I watched their interaction for a few minutes before focusing back on the screen. Frustrated that I couldn't pin point the nagging familiarity I exited out of Natasha's application and turned my attention back to the residential floor plan I was working on.

Rotating the furniture for what seemed like the hundredth time I was frustrated that it wasn't laying out the way I'd thought it would. I was close, almost had everything figured out, but it still wasn't quite right. I glanced over at the conference room and realized the interview with Natasha was over and my dad was leaving the conference room.

Checking the time on my computer screen, I was a bit shocked at how quickly the interview was over. It was a pretty good indication that it either went really well or not so good. I knew my dad had a pretty good initial sense about people in general and could tell if someone was going to work out or not. That was one of the biggest reasons why our team was so solid. Most of our employees stayed and we didn't have constant turn over.

Natasha seemed sad or disappointed, it was hard to tell from the distance I was at. She shoved her laptop back in her bag and she couldn't seem to move quick enough out of the conference room. Her shoulders were slumped slightly but then half way toward the reception area she glanced over her shoulder and looked back. I wondered if she sensed me watching her. When she turned back around, she straightened her shoulders, and walked the rest of the way out with confidence; stopping for a quick moment to talk to my mom before she exited out the front doors.

Saving the file I was working on. I pushed back my chair and headed toward my dad's office. The door was open and he sat in his chair with his headset talking on the phone. He motioned me to come in and sit. Taking a seat in the guest chair in front of his desk I waited for him to finish his call.

The small conference table in the corner was still piled with rolls of plans, his desk had sketches and papers scattered across it. It was rare to ever see the surface, but he knew where everything was at. The low filing cabinet credenza behind his desk was about the only clean surface and displayed a couple of framed pictures of our family. The back wall had his degree and licenses framed and hung. There was also a framed photo of the very first project he'd ever done completely by himself from the ground up.

A few more minutes passed while I listened to the one-sided conversation, I knew it was one of the projects that we had under construction. Hanging up the phone he sighed as he pulled the headset off and set it on the desk.

"More layout issues?" I asked.

"I don't understand how we got to this point. How hard is it to follow the dimensions we laid out? We've got one whole side of the offices laid out incorrectly. The angles are too steep and everything else now isn't lining up. There's over two feet of difference. That's not acceptable. The contractor is working with the sub to figure out where the break is, but I'll have to stop by after lunch to walk it with them."

"I'm sure you'll get it figured out. You always do." I smiled. I knew my dad and thankfully he had a pretty even temper. Even when he was his most frustrated on a project, he held his cool and worked through the issues. It had earned him loyal contractors and clients over the years and kept our workload full.

"How's the floor plan coming for the Heely residence?"

"It's almost done. I'll be ready for them to come in and review by the end of the week. Hopefully this will be our last revision. I have about ten different layouts now. Each time they come in they think of some new thing that they *have* to have, and of course it's completely different from what they previously *had* to have."

My dad chuckled. "That's usually how it goes."

"I know, but it doesn't make it any less frustrating."

"Most times they don't know what they want until they see it. You've been through this before. Sometimes you get the lucky project that you layout once and the client loves it and you move to the next step. But that's usually not the norm."

"I know. I think this revision might be the one though. It's really coming together and flows well, but there's still a couple things that need tweaking."

"Bring it in when you get it finished. I'd like to see it. What else is up?"

"Your interview was super short. I thought she was the one out of the three we have coming in you felt the best about."

"She is. Unless the other two completely blow me away with their interview she's the one we'll be bringing on this summer."

"How'd you figure it out so quickly? You were barely in that room with her."

"Sometimes you just know Troy. Her recommendations are top notch. She had a good presence about her, and her portfolio is one of the best

I've seen in a really long time. Her projects show a refinement that you rarely see in a first-year student's work. She's got a natural talent."

"Oh, okay she seemed kind of disappointed when she left, I wasn't sure."

"Disappointed?"

"Yeah, at least that was what it looked like to me."

"I told her she should be really proud of her work and that I'd let her know by the end of the week what our decision would be."

"Maybe she just thought you were being nice. It was a super short interview."

"The other two candidates will be in tomorrow. One in the morning. One in the afternoon. We'll know for sure by then."

"So, an off the subject question, did she seem familiar to you at all?"

"No, not really. Why?"

"I'm not sure. I just got this feeling like I've met her or something before."

There was a long pause while I could see my dad thinking about my question. His voice lowered almost to a whisper. "She is the same age as your sister, maybe that's it?"

The change in my dad's voice was immediate. I was surprised he even mentioned her, no one ever talked about her anymore.

"Maybe, maybe that's all it is. I was just curious how it went. Well, I better get back to work. I'll bring in the plan as soon as I'm finished with it." I rushed out of the office back to the silence of my space. Shoving memories and thoughts of my sister aside.

CHAPTER FIVE

~ Natasha ~

Sitting in my car I rested my head on the steering wheel and tried to push away all my emotions. So what if I didn't get the summer internship? I'd go home for the summer, no big deal. I'd get to see my best friends and maybe it would be easier to shove aside everything that had happened over the weekend by being far away.

I tried to convince myself, but the honest truth was I wanted that internship. I didn't realize how much until I'd walked into that office. I felt a pull there I'd never felt before. There wasn't anything I could do at this point. If it was meant to be then it would happen.

As the car engine rumbled, I glanced at the office one more time before pulling onto the street. Knowing I was going to be up late working on my final project I swung by the local Starbucks for a caffeine pick me up. Parking nearby on the street I locked my car and walked inside.

As always it was full of college students studying and most of the tables were filled. I scanned the room while I waited to place my order but didn't find anyone I knew. Pulling out my phone I checked through my emails, one from Bailey caught my attention and I opened it as I moved forward in line.

Scanning through her tales of school made me smile. I was so focused on the email that the deep voice and touch to my back almost sent me through the roof. I choked back a scream, spun quickly, and found myself staring up into Caleb's laughing face.

"Geez Natasha, I didn't mean to scare you. It's your turn to order." He chuckled as he pointed to the counter where the barista waited for me.

"Sorry, I'm tired and I was reading an email from a friend. Guess I had zoned out." I smiled weakly and turned to place my order. After paying I sat down at one of the two available tables to wait for my order. I watched Caleb as he ordered and then sauntered over to my table.

"Can I join you?" he asked motioning to the empty chair across from me.

"Sure, but I'm not staying. I'm grabbing my coffee and then headed back to the dorm to work on my final project."

"I came back to your desk last night but you were gone already. Is everything okay?"

His eyes searched mine and I tried to calm my racing heart. I wasn't sure if I was excited that he'd sought me out, or if I was afraid. My senses were still messed up from the weekend. I didn't think Caleb could have been the one. It just didn't make sense. I really needed to get my head on straight and focus on school. I'd worked too hard all year to let everything fall apart this close to the end of the school year.

Once more I shoved my fear and my anxiety down deeper inside, stomping on it and burying it. If I didn't think about it, if I never thought about it again then I could just pretend it never happened. It wasn't like I had any memories of it happening. I slammed the door shut on my thoughts and told myself to forget it. To never ever talk about it again. Focus on school and not look back. I could do it. I had to. There was no other option.

"I'm good, thanks Caleb. My project is coming along, I just worked on it for a while in my dorm room."

"Did you get the rest of your model finished?"

"No, that's the last thing I have to do, the rest is pretty much finished though. I'll be relieved after our final presentations are done."

"One year down and four more to go."

I laughed, "Thanks for the encouragement. Looks like my order is done. I'll see you around Caleb."

"Any chance I can catch a ride back to campus? I walked over."

"Oh. Yeah that's fine I can do that."

Caleb's bright smile lit up his face giving him a playful boyish look. "Thanks, I'd appreciate it."

Caleb's order was on the counter next to mine when we reached it. I grabbed my coffee and my lemon loaf while Caleb picked up his coffee and followed me to the door. He reached around me and pushed it open allowing me to walk through in front of him.

"Thanks. My car is across the street." I gestured to where it was parked.

I walked quickly to my car. Caleb fell in step with me. I didn't know what to say to him. All year long I'd wanted to get enough courage up to ask him out. But deep down I knew that what I really wanted was for him to be the one to make the first move. I was a hopeless romantic. I wanted romance. The fairy tale guy to come in and sweep me off my feet. Wasn't that what was supposed to happen? So, I never said anything all year long. And here I was about to get in my car alone with him.

I was a jumble of nerves and now I didn't know what I wanted, but I also told myself it was just a ride back to school. It wasn't like we were on a date or anything. We reached my car and I unlocked the doors.

Caleb dwarfed my passenger seat, filling the car. I was surprised his head didn't hit the ceiling. I hadn't realized how tiny my car really was. Placing my coffee in the cup holder I tossed my purse on the backseat floorboard, buckled my seatbelt and started the car.

"So, do you have plans this summer?" he asked.

"Not sure yet. I just finished an internship interview with a local firm. If that doesn't work out, then I'll go home to Riverview for the summer."

"Which firm? Was it my dad's company? Wilson & Associates? There aren't that many local firms."

I looked at him, stunned. "How did I not know your family had a firm?" My hand lay still on the gearshift. "It wasn't Wilson & Associates where I had my interview."

"We do internships every summer. You should apply. I don't think the slots have been filled yet for this summer. I can put in a good word for you. I thought you knew about the firm. Most of the students and faculty do. My dad went through the same program years ago. He's been practicing locally since he got his license."

Backing out of the parking stall my head was spinning. Maybe I wouldn't have to go back home for the summer after all. "That's awesome, yes I'd like to apply, that might give me other options."

"Who did you interview with?"

"DeLuca Architects."

"Forget DeLuca Architects. I can get you in at our office we have a better program and pay structure anyway."

"I'm pretty sure it isn't going to pan out, the interview was super short."

"I'll talk to my dad tonight and get you the info. I know you'd be a perfect fit in our office."

"How come you never mentioned it before?"

"I thought you knew; we post on the boards near the end of the school year with the job listings."

"I've been so focused on my projects and getting through the year, I never put two and two together." I glanced at him sideways, kicking myself for not paying more attention. It totally made sense now why his projects were always so amazing. He'd been working in the field this whole time. "Did you want me to drop you off somewhere specific on campus?"

"No. Where ever you are parking, I can walk from there."

I circled around the parking lot until I finally found a spot and pulled in. Shutting my car off. I grabbed my coffee and got out. I opened the back door to pull out my purse and laptop bag. By the time I shut the door Caleb had walked around the car and was standing at the rear fender.

"I'll walk with you. Do you need any help?"

"No, I'm good. Thanks though." I shouldered my purse and laptop bag, locked my car and started walking toward my dorm with Caleb at my side.

"I'll be in the studio most of tonight. If you need any help, come find me."

"Thanks, I'm not sure yet where I'm going to work. I got a lot done last night. But model building isn't as easy to do in the dorm." We reached the building and I stopped on the sidewalk looking up at Caleb. "I appreciate your help. You've been really great to me all year."

"I'm happy to help. I've told you several times you've got a natural talent. Do you have my cell number? You can always text or call me too."

"Um, no I don't." I pulled my cell from my purse as he rattled off his number and I returned by giving him my number.

"Perfect, I'll get you the info on the summer positions. Thanks for the ride! I'll see you around Natasha."

I stood at the side entry door and watched dumbfounded as Caleb walked down the sidewalk, not sure I believed that had all just happened. Shaking my head, I pushed open the door and walked to my dorm room. I was exhausted, I hoped my coffee would kick in quick. I had a lot to finish.

CHAPTER SIX

~ *Natasha* ~

A car alarm was going off, and it sounded like it was right in my ear. I rolled over pulling the blanket over my head, and tried to block it out. Why didn't someone turn it off? I just wanted to sleep. It felt like I'd only gotten to bed a few minutes ago. The continuous beeping persisted until in my haze I realized it was my phone alarm going off.

My brain was fuzzy. I'd basically been up the last twenty-four hours finishing my physical model for my final presentation that I had to give later this afternoon. It had turned out better than I'd thought and I was excited to present the entire project, but I was exhausted.

I fumbled with the phone, my eyes blurry and burning as I shut off the alarm. I weighed my options. How long could I push my alarm before I had to be up for my class this morning? Did I really need to wash my hair? Nope, I'd throw it up in a messy bun or something. I needed sleep a lot worse than spending extra time getting ready.

Decision made I added an extra thirty minutes to my alarm and set it back on the table as I rolled over snuggling further into my blankets. Sleep. I just needed a bit more sleep. I felt myself just drifting off when my phone began to ring.

"Who the hell is calling me this early?" I mumbled as I rolled back over to read the number displayed. The number looked vaguely familiar but I was too exhausted to figure it out. Grabbing it, I answered.

"Hello." I tried to sound at least partially conscious, even though I was still half asleep.

"Natasha, this is Thomas DeLuca."

The deep voice on the other end of the phone, was like a splash of cold water to my face. I was awake and alert. Sitting up quickly I held the phone tighter in my hand. My heart started pounding.

"Good morning Mr. DeLuca."

"Thomas, please. Mr. DeLuca is so formal. I wanted to call and let you know that we've chosen you for the internship position this summer. We'd like to have you start as soon as you're finished with finals next week."

"Really? I'm speechless. Thank you so much! I'm honored to be selected for the position."

"We look forward to seeing you soon. Give Camille a call later this afternoon and she'll get you scheduled in for your first day."

"Okay, thank you again for this amazing opportunity."

"You're welcome, we'll see you soon. Bye Natasha."

"Good bye."

I clicked end on my phone and stared at it, still in utter disbelief. How had that happened? I had been so sure I hadn't gotten the job when I left the interview. Immediately energized, I jumped out of bed and got ready for the day.

A HEALING TOUCH

My model and presentation boards were lying on my desk. I sat in my tall studio chair, feet propped on the footrest, my legs anxiously bouncing up and down. I was next to present and my stomach was in complete knots. Once I got started, I always relaxed, but those minutes right before I had to present were the most nerve wracking ever.

A hand on my shoulder startled me. My foot slipped, almost causing me to lose my balance on the chair. A strong arm stabled me as I looked up into Caleb's face.

"Man, you are really jumpy lately." He said as he lifted his hand from my shoulder and I was able to breathe again.

"I'm running through my project in my head. What to say, what not to say. Presentations are the hardest. You never know what piece they might rip apart."

"You're going to do awesome. Your project is really good Natasha. Don't stress."

"Thanks, but that's easier said than done." I tried to smile. My heart was starting to finally slow down. "What are you doing here, don't you have your presentation soon?"

"I stopped in to watch your presentation and also to let you know I talked to my dad about the summer internship program we have. He said the position is all yours."

"That's amazing Caleb. Really, I can't thank you enough for talking to him. But DeLuca Architects called this morning and I got the job there. I was totally surprised, I thought there was no way I was going to get it."

"Just turn it down. Come work for us. You'll have more opportunities with us, and it'll be more fun. I promise."

"I kinda already told them yes. I really appreciate your help though, it really means a lot."

"Wow, I can't believe you're turning this down."

"I'm sorry Caleb. I am grateful for the opportunity, and your help this year has been amazing. I really do value your input." My name being called pulled my attention to the review panel. "It's my turn. I've got to set up."

Sliding off my chair I carefully grabbed my model and boards and positioned everything for my presentation. Once I was ready to go, I checked through my notes one last time, took a deep breath and looked at the panel of architects that would be critiquing my project.

A couple had been here before, but there were two new ones that had been super rough on my other classmates that had already presented. All I could do was hope for the best. There wasn't any going back now.

Glancing past them, I caught Caleb's eye as he stood arms crossed over his chest while he leaned against my desk. He's expression was unreadable. Gone was the carefree smile I was used to seeing.

Shaking off my uneasiness, I started with my concept, and before I knew it, I was done and waiting for the most difficult part. Either the panel was going to like it or not.

My eyes drifted from each panelist and then to the back of the room when I realized that Caleb was gone. I hadn't seen him leave and had no idea if he'd left right away or if he'd seen my entire presentation. Before I could really think about it the questions started coming and I had to focus on answering them.

I was still on cloud nine, I couldn't believe I had the highest rated project from my class. For the first time in days I felt my normal self. Unlocking the door to my dorm room I practically skipped into the room, catching Justine off guard. She sat propped up on her bed her text book in her lap, highlighter in hand.

"There's my girl. It must have gone well?"

"It was amazing Justine! Only a couple minor things that they said needed work, but the rest of it, they loved! By the time everyone was done they did an overview and they picked mine as the best project! Can you believe it?" I asked as I set down my model and boards and shut the door behind me.

Justine chuckled. "Um, yes, actually I can. You worked really hard on it. I know I don't know all the terms and stuff, or all the other projects, but what I saw of yours was really good."

"And guess who called this morning?"

"I have no idea."

"DeLuca Architects. I got the job!"

"I knew it!" Justine tossed her textbook aside and jumped from the bed, pulling me into a bear hug. "Congrats Natasha! I think we need to go out and celebrate tonight! Neither of us have class tomorrow. It's time to have some fun!"

Justine sat across from me in the small quaint booth. She continued to chatter away as we finished our dinner. She had picked a local hangout with amazing food and Thursday's through Saturday nights the small dance floor was packed mostly with the local college kids. I pushed the last of my meal around on the plate, full and not able to take another bite.

The lights dimmed and the music got louder as several people began moving toward the dance floor. I was ready to go. The darkened atmosphere and music was beginning to make me jumpy. Reaching for the check that our waitress had left on the table a few minutes previous, Justine was a split second quicker and smacked my hand.

"No way, this is my treat. We're celebrating for you; you're not paying for dinner."

Laughing, I conceded. "Okay, thank you. The food was awesome as always. I think this is one of my favorite spots in town."

The music was thumping through the restaurant now, and more people were moving toward the dance floor. Justine pulled cash out and set the leather folder back on the table.

"Ready?" she asked.

"Yes. Let's go."

"One dance?" She grinned. Her face lighting up.

"Um, can we just go? I'm not really up for dancing."

Justine slid from the booth and dragged me to my feet. "Come on, one dance. We're celebrating. Remember?"

She was so persistent when she got her mind set to something. She reminded me a lot of one of my best friends back home, Mia. The two of them even looked a bit alike. It was kind of uncanny when I thought of it. Maybe that's why I felt like I'd known her forever and we'd just clicked. I didn't resist and let her drag me onto the dance floor, where the music switched to the next song.

"I love this song!" she screamed as she began moving to the beat.

Laughing I joined her, telling myself to just relax and let go. We danced through that song and the next. Sweat was beginning to bead on my forehead and at my neck. I was losing myself in the song. It was one of my favorites.

Closing my eyes as I moved, I focused on the music, losing myself to the rhythm. I felt someone run their hand over my backside as they whispered my name in my ear. The hair on the back of my neck stood on end. It was like a bucket of cold water had been tossed on me, snapping me out of my happy place. My eyes sprung open as I spun around but no one was there.

Panic consumed me, and I was having trouble breathing. The heat from the bodies moving around me was making me feel faint. I needed fresh air and couldn't get out of the restaurant fast enough. Pushing my way through the crowded dance floor I practically ran from the room to the front door.

Once outside I stopped to get my breath and quickly looked around me. It was dark out, but the sidewalks were still full of people. Moving away from the front door, I walked to the painted steel bench that was nearby. I sat down and leaned over. My arms crossed, resting on my knees I continued to take deep breaths and tried to calm my racing heart.

What was wrong with me? But I knew the answer. I'm sure someone had just bumped into me. It probably wasn't intentional. Or maybe it didn't even happen and I totally imagined it, but I could have sworn someone had whispered my name too.

This was not good. Now I was hearing things in my head. Pressure on my shoulder had me sitting up quickly. My purse in hand. I was ready to swing it.

"Whoa, sorry! Are you okay Natasha?"

Setting my purse back in my lap I looked up into the face of Troy DeLuca. I let out the air I'd been holding. "Um, yeah. I'll be fine. I just got a little overheated in there."

"I saw you run from the restaurant. I wanted to make sure you were okay."

"It was nothing. I'm okay, just got a little claustrophobic in there, and needed some air."

"Are you with someone?"

"My roommate. Crap, I didn't tell her where I was going. I better get back in. She's going to be worried when she realizes I'm gone."

"I'll walk you back inside."

He reached his hand out to me and I stared. My heart started pounding again and I couldn't shake the panic that was overcoming me. Minutes passed or maybe it was just seconds. I was still so shaken I knew I wasn't thinking clearly.

I finally placed my left hand in his strong, warm one. I felt the gentle tug as he helped me up. As soon as I was on my feet, I quickly pulled my hand back. It felt like it an electric shock had traveled up my arm. Troy waved his hand toward the door of the restaurant.

"After you."

A HEALING TOUCH

Putting one foot in front of the next, I walked back toward the entry door, almost as if on autopilot. I noticed that Troy had guided me to the inside of the sidewalk while he walked closest to the traffic. It was so subtle; I didn't even really notice he had done it.

I snuck a glance to my side and up at the profile of Troy. He really was handsome. Rugged. Strong cheekbones. A bit of dark stubble covered his face. As I studied him, he caught me staring and smiled. My face flushed, and I snapped my head forward.

"So, how'd your final presentation go? Are you ready to get started at work?"

"It went really well. Thank you. And yes, I'm excited. It's an amazing opportunity."

"We've got a lot going on this summer. You should be able to get lots of first-hand experience."

The doors of the restaurant opened and Justine came flying out. "Natasha! Oh. My. God. You scared the living crap out of me! I turned around and you were gone! I thought maybe you'd gone to the bathroom, but when I didn't find you there, I was starting to freak out."

"I'm sorry. I got hot and came out for fresh air. I should have told you."

Justine threw her arms around me and hugged me tight. "Are you okay?"

"Yes, I'm fine. Troy here was just escorting me back inside."

Justine pulled away from me and then thoroughly looked Troy up and down. I wanted to just shrivel up and die. She was so obvious.

"Do I pass inspection?" he asked as he extended his hand to Justine. "Troy DeLuca, nice to meet you. I'm assuming you're the roommate?"

Justine took his hand and shook it. "Yes, I'm Justine. DeLuca? As in DeLuca Architects?"

"Very nice to meet you Justine, and yes that's the one."

"Nice to meet you as well. Natasha, are you ready to go?"

"Yes." Looking up into the smiling eyes of Troy I was having a hard time assembling my thoughts. I was still rattled from earlier. "Thanks Troy, I'll see you next week at work."

"Have a good rest of your evening. Ladies."

Justine grabbed my arm, interlacing hers with mine and spun me around as we walked toward the parking lot. "You did not say anything about what a hottie he was!"

"Shhh!!" I glanced over my shoulder to make sure Troy hadn't overheard her. Thankfully, it looked like he'd gone back inside the restaurant as the door was just closing.

"He's the boss's son Justine. I have to work with him."

"And your point?"

"Seriously? I'm not ready for any type of relationship right now. I'm pretty messed up in the head. I freaked out there on the dance floor because I thought someone touched me and whispered in my ear. I'm losing it. I snapped and couldn't breathe. I had to get out of there."

"Oh love, I'm so sorry. You were there and then you were gone. You seriously about gave me a heart attack."

"It's getting late. Let's get back to the dorm. I think I'm done celebrating for the night."

CHAPTER SEVEN

~ *Natasha* ~

Staring in the mirror, I took in my reflection. Thankfully, the bags under my eyes had disappeared after finally getting some sleep the last couple of days. I tucked in my fitted black and white pinstripe top into the black pencil skirt I had chosen for my first day of work. I adjusted my earrings and necklace, and slipped on my black ballet flats.

I was ready, or at least as ready as I could be. I was nervous and excited all at once, wondering how things would be in the real world. Working on real projects instead of just made up projects that I'd been doing all year.

Grabbing my purse and locking the dorm room behind me I made my way down the corridor to exit the dorm. It was still cool as I walked across the parking lot to my car, almost chilly and I contemplated going back for a sweater. Checking the time on my phone, I decided there wasn't enough time. I didn't want to risk being late my first day. Hopefully it would warm up a bit and that the office wouldn't be an ice box. Worst case I'd come back during lunch and grab something.

The drive was quick and before I knew it, I was pushing open the front doors of the office ready to start this new adventure in my life. Camille was already at the front desk. Her bright smile lit up her face as she greeted me.

"Good Morning, Natasha. Welcome. I believe that Troy is going to be the one showing you around today and getting you situated. I'll take you back to your new desk and you can get settled in."

I followed her as she walked briskly through the open office space. The center of the office was open with eight "L" shaped workstations. They were in clusters of two anchoring each corner with a big open table in the middle.

Camille guided me to the far back group. Along the back wall there were three offices with full glass walls. The open workstations faced the offices which allowed for views to the outside through the exterior windows. A woman sat at the adjacent desk, focused on her computer screen as we approached.

"Kelsey, I'd like you to meet our new intern, Natasha. She'll be working with you and Troy on the Heely Residence."

Kelsey stood up to shake my hand. I hadn't realized how tall she was. Her smile lit up her face.

"Welcome Natasha. I'm glad we've finally got another female working in here. We need more female input. I get overruled all the time."

I liked her immediately. My racing heart was starting to finally slow down. I still couldn't believe all of this was really happening.

Kelsey returned to her chair as I walked around the two desks and sat down in my new workstation. Camille placed a paper on the surface as I adjusted my chair.

"This is a list of the programs, your email account, file info, and everything you should need to get started. If you have any questions just ask.

"As I mentioned your main project will be assisting Kelsey and Troy, but you could be pulled onto other projects as needed. The break room is kept stocked full of goodies. You are welcome to help yourself to anything in there or you can bring your own food in if you prefer. Several of us will go out for lunch or order in.

"We're pretty flexible. You'll need to make sure you always have steel-toed, puncture resistant shoes with you in your car. You never know when you'll need to go out to a construction site.

"We're also pretty casual, so nice slacks or even jeans with nice tops are okay, and are actually better in case you do end up on a jobsite. Skirts can get tricky. Open toed shoes aren't allowed on a construction site. It's just not safe."

"Okay, thanks. I'll make sure to get some new shoes right away."

"Perfect. Okay, I think you're set. I'll let you get settled in. Kelsey will help get your started."

"Thank you, Mrs. DeLuca."

"Camille, please, that's what everyone calls me around here. Same with Thomas and Troy. We're all on a first name basis." She smiled as she walked back to the reception area.

Kelsey leaned over our adjoining desk surfaces, her elbows bent with her chin resting on her hands. "I'm seriously so excited you are here!"

"Thanks, I'm excited to be here too. How long have you worked here?"

"Two years. I worked here my final year of school. I started just like you as an intern and then when I finished school they hired me full time. I'm trying to study for all my exams but I just can't get into it. Troy and I went through school together. He's always been so driven. Me, I love what I do, but not sure I want to go through all the licensing stuff. I kind of just like doing the drafting and helping with the design. At least for now. Maybe that will change down the road. But for now, I'm good."

"Oh, wow, that's cool. Are you and Troy dating?"

Kelsey's laugh was deep, her eyes crinkling at the corners. "Nah, I did have crush on him when we were in school. I mean just look at him. He's hot, and super talented. But we've never dated. Just became pretty good friends. We did a lot of group projects together in school. When I started working here it was a natural transition. Troy has never been one to date much. He really is a workaholic. He's very driven, focused, and usually pretty easy to work with. I will say though, he does have his days when he's super moody, and it's best to just stay clear of him when he's in a mood."

"Good to know. I hope you clue me in on those days."

"I've got your back. But I don't think I'll need to say anything. It's pretty obvious when he's having a bad day. I've only worked with Jordan on a couple projects. I have never been on a project with Thomas, so I don't have as much information on either of them. But for the most part, the work environment here is pretty easy going. Let me know when you get everything set up, and I'll go over your first assignment."

A HEALING TOUCH

Focused on my computer screen, I moved appliances around in different locations for the proposed kitchen layout I was working on. It felt like I was being watched. I tried to shake off the feeling and focus on this latest plan. It was finally coming together. I was in a groove and didn't want to break my concentration.

A touch to my shoulder about sent me shooting from my chair. I spun quickly, and in the process, caught the corner of the cup I had sitting on my desk. It was still half full of water, which promptly dumped over, splattering straight into my lap. A scream escaped, and I felt all eyes were on me. My face flushed as I frantically tried to brush the water off my lap.

"I'm so sorry!" Evan, one of the other designers that I had met earlier in the morning exclaimed. "You weren't responding to your name. I didn't mean to startle you."

I sighed, my skirt was soaking wet, but I knew it was my fault for being so clumsy. "It's okay. It's not your fault. I wasn't paying attention."

"Alex and I were going to lunch and wanted to know if you and Kelsey wanted to join us."

"I'm game." Kelsey replied as she saved her file and put her computer to sleep.

"I'm okay. I'll probably just go back to my dorm and change clothes."

"I'm sure it'll dry quick outside. It's pretty warm today." Evan stated.

"Maybe another time. Thanks for the invite though." I cringed as I could feel the moisture soaking through my skirt. Wet clothes were the worst.

"Okay. Next time. Come on Kelsey. Alex is buying today."

"Awesome, that's even better. I'm starving. Natasha, I can bring you back something if you'd like."

"No thanks, I'm good. I'll just grab something when I go change. I'll see you when I get back. I think I've got a layout that works we can go over this afternoon."

"Cool. I haven't had any luck with it. Too many requirements and not enough space. I can't wait to see what you've come up with."

I saved my work, grabbed my purse, my wet clothes clinging to me as I hurried out to the parking lot. Thankfully, my dorm wasn't too far of a drive. I'd be able to change and still have a few minutes to grab something to eat.

~ *Troy* ~

It had been a rough morning. I'd stopped by the messed-up office project to see how things were coming along. There were still layout issues that were beyond frustrating. I'd already gone over the adjustments with the superintendent, but the subcontractor was being stubborn and was not listening to direction. We were on a tight time schedule and didn't have time to waste on stupidity.

By the time I'd finally reached the office, half the morning was already over, and I'd completely forgotten about Natasha starting work today. Thankfully, Kelsey had gotten her settled in and started on a project. I'd check on them later. Kelsey and I worked well together and I was grateful that she was so easy going and willing to work with Natasha.

I caught myself more than once watching Natasha as she worked. Her desk faced my office, as did Kelsey's. The open plan made collaborating a lot easier than everyone in separate offices.

I still couldn't shake the nagging feeling that there was something familiar about Natasha. It was really starting to bug me but I couldn't nail it down. What was it that was causing this reaction? I'd had the same feeling the night I ran into her at the restaurant. Sighing I turned back to the set of plans that I was redlining.

The door to my office was open as it usually was. A scream suddenly shattered the constant hum of work and activity in the office, startling me. I quickly stood up and looked out over the office to see what had happened.

Scanning the open office area, I realized the scream had come from Natasha. Evan stood next to her, shaking his head. Before I could leave my office, Natasha had already grabbed her things and practically ran out the door.

"Evan, can you come here, please?"

"Hey, Troy. What's up?" Evan asked as he entered my office.

"What was all that out there? What made Natasha scream and why did she bail so quickly?"

"It was my fault, I startled her. We were going to head out for lunch. I was just asking if she wanted to join us. When she wasn't responding, I tapped her on the shoulder. Then she screamed and jumped. In the process, she knocked over her glass of water and it spilled all down the front of her. I told her I was sorry. I didn't mean to scare her. She was really focused on her computer. She said she was going back to her dorm to change and then she'd be back."

"Oh, did she seem okay?"

"I guess, I mean I'm sure having water all down the front of you isn't the most comfortable."

"Okay, thanks."

Sitting back at my desk I watched as the group left for lunch. I'd grab something later. I wanted to finish up marking up the changes to the Heely Elevations so those could be updated before they arrived for their meeting at the end of the week.

I sensed movement before I caught it out of the corner of my eye. Everyone else was still gone at lunch and the office was empty except for me and Natasha. Glancing over my computer screen, I realized she had changed clothes and was now in more casual attire than she had been earlier. She settled into her chair never looking up.

Watching her for a few minutes the overwhelming feeling of déjà vu hit me again, but for the life of me I still couldn't figure out what is was.

While both Kelsey and her desks faced my office, it was like she was in her own world. I don't think she even realized I was there in the office. Observing her for a few more minutes I finally pushed back my chair. The noise caught Natasha's attention and her head snapped up her eyes catching mine. She almost looked like a deer that had just been caught in headlights.

Leaving my office, I walked over to the front of her desk. Her eyes followed every move I made. She finally seemed to calm down as I reached her desk.

"Sorry about Evan. He's sometimes a little oblivious. How's everything else going on your first day?"

"It's going good. Kelsey has me working on changes to the kitchen layout. I think I've got it about worked out with their most recent requests. She showed me all the other previous plans that you guys had gone through and the list of requirements for the space."

"Cool. Bring it up. Let's see what you've got." I walked around the desk, grabbed one of the guest chairs, and pulled it up next to Natasha. "Okay, walk me through what you've got here and why you've done what you've done."

I listened to Natasha as she talked through her plan, her logic, and the reasoning behind her design. The layout that she'd been able to squeeze into the space she had to work with was impressive. My dad had been right, not like he usually wasn't, but she had natural talent.

We'd spent a lot of time on the kitchen layout and in just a couple hours this morning she'd worked out the kinks and pulled the design together. I suggested a couple minor tweaks and asked her to start blocking out the interior cabinet elevations so that the client could get a better feel for the layout.

After the lousy morning I'd had, the afternoon was finally turning around. I stood up, pushing back the chair I'd been sitting in. "Nice work, Natasha. Keep it up."

She looked up at me almost shocked. "Um, thanks Troy." With a slight smile, she turned quickly back to her computer screen and I walked back to my office.

~ *Natasha* ~

Troy's compliment made me smile. I couldn't help it. It felt good when things laid out and worked. I really enjoyed the challenge. Solving the puzzle. The small tweaks that he suggested were just what the design was missing.

Saving the plan, I started blocking out the interior elevations. I flipped through the folder of kitchen design inspiration that the client had left as I refined the elevations, adding small pieces of detail.

The afternoon flew by, and before I knew it, the day was over and everyone was packing up to leave for the day. I saved my work and was shutting down my computer when a text came through on my phone.

Caleb
Congrats on your first
day of work. Want to
grab a coffee?

Staring at my phone I wasn't really sure what to say back. Actually, I was quite surprised Caleb had even texted me. I hadn't seen him since the day of my presentation when he'd acted so weird after I'd told him

A HEALING TOUCH

I'd gotten the job here. I held the phone in my hand debating what to reply back.

> Natasha
> Thanks, but I'm tired. I'm just going to go back to the dorm.

> Caleb
> One coffee, I wanted to apologize for the other day.

I was torn. I was probably making more out of his outburst and it probably didn't mean anything. He had been such a huge help all year on my projects and I probably wouldn't have done as well on my final presentation without his input.

Deep down inside though, I just wanted to be alone. Justine had left the day before to spend two weeks at her parents before summer classes started, so I'd have the room to myself until she returned.

> Natasha
> It's okay. I appreciate the apology. Another time, okay?

> Caleb
> Sure

Grabbing my purse, I walked out of the office. Camille had already left earlier, so the lobby was empty as I pushed through the glass doors and headed to my car. Clouds had moved in since lunch. The air was moist, but not yet raining. I hurried across the parking lot, slid behind the wheel, and just as I shut the door, the skies opened up and rain pelted my windows. I hadn't paid much attention to the weather, but rain in the northwest was a pretty common thing. It was so different than what I was used to having when I grew up in Southern California.

The drive back to the dorm was quick. It was nice that I didn't have far to go every day. The rain had lightened by the time I parked. Unfortunately, I'd left my umbrella inside so I'd have to dash to the door to avoid getting soaked. I really wasn't in the mood for a second set of clothes in one day.

My phone rang as I unlocked the door to my dorm room. Grabbing it from my purse, I pushed through the door. The caller ID read "Mia".

"Hey Mia." I answered as I tossed my purse and keys on the desk. Toeing my shoes off as I walked across the room to the bed.

"Don't 'Hey Mia me.' Why are you not home for the summer?"

I sighed. I knew this call was coming. I was actually surprised my best friend hadn't raked me over the coals before now. Mia and I had practically grown up together in Riverview, California. "I told you I was interviewing for some jobs."

"Um, yeah, but you failed to say they were up there in Oregon! I thought you had some interviews down here."

"Oh, whoops. Sorry. Things have been kind of crazy up here with finals and everything and then getting the job."

"Tasha, what is going on? You don't sound like yourself."

"What do you mean?"

"You sound different. Come on, what's going on? We've been friends forever. I know you. This isn't like you."

"I'm fine Mia. I'm just tired. The architecture program is pretty intense. You know that. I've been telling you all along how crazy things have been."

"Yeah, but something is different. You sound different. Something's wrong. I can feel it. And you said you were coming home this summer."

"Mia, nothing's wrong. In fact, it's really good. I really love the firm I'm working for and I had a really amazing first day."

"Are you sure? Maybe Bailey and I should come up for a visit then this summer. Are you planning to come home at all?"

"I'm not sure if I'm going to make it home. I didn't really discuss taking any time off this summer when I got hired. Then after I realized I was going to be staying, I went ahead and signed up for a summer school class. That way my fall semester won't be as packed, and so that I could stay in the dorm."

"Tasha! Why would you do that? You need a break. You're going to burn yourself out."

"I'll be okay. It's just a basic general ed class that I have to take. You know me, I always like to stay busy. So, tell me how are things with you and Dylan? Any other wild adventures that you two have been on?"

"Things are good. Really good. I still am in shock some days at how lucky I am to have him."

Mia's love for Dylan was so obvious every time she talked about him. I knew that it would take the questions off of me once she started talking about him. Mia was way too observant. She always had a second sense when things were wrong.

Growing up together, I could never hide things from her, which was another reason why I didn't want to go back home during the summer. I knew that Mia would take one look at me and she'd know something was up. I needed time to hide, to hide everything deep down inside me so that no one could see it.

Mia continued to update me on all the latest news from home and finally after close to thirty minutes she had to run. "Tasha, you know you can tell me anything right?"

"Yes, Mia, and I love you for it. But I promise I'm fine, just tired, and I really am excited for this new job okay?"

"Okay. But you better come home sometime this summer!"

"I'll see what I can do alright?" I laughed.

"Bye, Tasha."

"Bye, Mia. Tell Dylan hello for me."

"I will."

Ending the call. I tossed the phone onto my bed as I pulled a change of clothes out of the closet. Curling up on my bed in a comfy pair of leggings and an oversized t-shirt. I opened up my kindle app on my iPad, and for the first time in months I was reading for enjoyment and not for an assignment. Reading was a love of mine that I hadn't had time for in far too long. It

A HEALING TOUCH

wasn't long before I couldn't keep my eyes open. Setting my alarm, I decided it was going to be an early night.

CHAPTER EIGHT

~ *Natasha* ~

The week flew by. I couldn't believe it was already Friday, and I'd finished my first week of work. I'd loved every minute of it. The work was challenging and I was learning more every day. Everyone was super nice and helpful and the work environment was relaxed but intense. I straightened up my desk, and started to close down my computer.

I had no plans for the weekend and I was totally okay with that. My plan was to decompress from finals and my first week of work. Justine was still at her parents but would be back late Sunday night. She was taking a full load for the summer. So that I could stay in the dorm with her I had registered last minute for a basic English class that wouldn't take up too much time in the evenings after work.

"Hey Natasha. What are you doing after work?" Kelsey asked.

"Nothing. Probably going to read and go to bed. I'm boring. I know."

"It's Friday night! Come on you have to at least come out to dinner with us. It's a ritual. Every Friday night after work a bunch of us go grab dinner. Come on it will be fun."

I was torn. A small part, a very, very small part, wanted to go out with everyone. I'd really enjoyed getting to know everyone over the week. But the stronger part of me just wanted quiet and solace. I was still jumpy and I hated the uneasiness that had settled inside me.

"I'm not sure, Kelsey. Maybe next week?"

"But you don't have any other plans tonight, right?"

"No"

"And you need to eat dinner somewhere, right?"

"I was just going to grab something on my way back to the dorm."

"Come on, Natasha. It will be fun. I promise. It's just dinner."

Kelsey's smiling brown eyes bore into mine, quite a lot like one of my best friends, Mia. It was so hard to say no to them. They had a way to talk you into everything. "Okay, fine. Just dinner and then I'm out."

"Yay! You can follow me over to the restaurant. It's a great Italian place around the corner."

~———~

When we reached the restaurant, the hostess greeted Kelsey and waved her to the back of the large dining room. "Your usual table is ready. You can head back."

"Your usual table?" I asked, grinning.

"I told you, it's a ritual. We do this almost every Friday night after work. They know us in here and always have a table ready for us. Come on, the food is amazing."

I followed Kelsey as she weaved between the tables to a large table tucked in a recessed niche at the back allowing for some privacy. Evan and Alex were both already at the table with two girls I hadn't met before.

Kelsey quickly introduced me to Jennifer, who was Evan's wife, and Alyssa, who was Alex's fiancé. Kelsey sat across the table from the two couples and I sat next to Kelsey. There were two more empty seats next to me.

"Is there anyone else coming?" I asked Kelsey.

"I'm not sure. Troy usually comes. Jordan, Nicolas and Camille come sometimes, but they aren't as regular about it. Jordan has three kids all under the age of five so he doesn't get out much."

Jennifer and Alyssa were chatting away about wedding preparations while I scanned the menu, trying to decide what to order. I was so focused on looking through the menu, I didn't even notice the chair next to me was being pulled out. Looking up, I expected to see the waitress, but instead I was looking up into the handsome face of Troy.

"I wasn't sure if you were going to make it this week." Kelsey stated as she leaned slightly behind me to talk to Troy.

"I figured since it was Natasha's first week on the job, she should get the full office welcome."

As Troy slid into his chair, my nerves were on high alert. I hated this new feeling I had of wanting to run. I could feel my heart start to race and it was getting harder to keep my breathing steady, but I refused to make a fool out of myself. I would stick it out, no matter how uncomfortable I was. The words on the menu were starting to blur. Closing my eyes for a split second I tried to rein in my panic that had suddenly overcome me and I had no idea why.

Taking a deep breath, I opened my eyes and focused, as my heart began to slow back to its normal pace. Troy's voice broke my concentration and I realized he had been repeating my name. My face flushed immediately as I looked up.

"Um what?" I asked.

"The waitress was asking what you'd like to drink," Troy responded.

"Oh, sorry. I'll have a diet coke please."

Kelsey got the same and then leaned over, pointing to the menu. "Any of these are amazing. Actually, pretty much anything on the menu is worth getting. The eggplant parmesan is my favorite though, and the bruschetta appetizer is the best in town if you'd like to split it with me."

"Sure, that sounds good. Thanks."

Troy and Evan started talking about the office building that they were working on and all the current construction issues. I listened quietly while I studied the menu. After figuring out what I was having, I set my menu down and focused on the conversation.

I hoped that I'd get to visit the construction site while it was still being built. The entire process was so intriguing. I had never realized how much problem solving was involved even after the plans were done. Each day I was learning more and more and it reinforced that I had selected the right profession. I really enjoyed it, at least everything I'd been exposed to so far.

Dinner flew by, and before I knew it the table was cleared, and Troy had snagged the bill. I was glad that Kelsey had dragged me along. I'd enjoyed getting to know everyone a little better, it was different being outside of the office. The food was also as good as she had said and I didn't have to figure out what I was going to eat for dinner.

The background music was getting louder and that's when I realized that there was a dance floor in the back corner. A DJ had set up, the lights were dimming, and several people had already gathered in the area. My heart was starting to beat faster and I knew it was time for me to make my exit.

"Well, I guess I better be headed out." Setting my napkin on the table, I pushed back my chair as I glanced over at Troy. "Thank you for dinner. I'll see everyone on Monday."

"Wait, you can't leave now. Let's go dance for a while. It's Friday night and it's still early," Kelsey pleaded.

"Maybe another time." I smiled trying not to sound unappreciative.

"I'm going to hold you to that," Kelsey stated as I stood up.

""Night everyone. Have a great weekend."

"I'll walk you out," Troy stated as he pushed back his chair.

"I'm okay, really. Go ahead and stay with everyone, I'll be fine."

"I've got some things I need to do anyways."

Grabbing my purse off the back of my chair, I turned and quickly walked back to the front entry. I could feel Troy's presence behind me. Once we reached the hostess station, he told them goodbye and then he was in front of me pushing the door open for me to pass through.

"Thanks," I practically whispered as I passed him. I immediately felt awkward, unsure of what to say.

Once through the doors, I fumbled through my purse in search of my keys and found myself running straight into a human wall. The grip on my arm stabilizing me was strong and my body immediately reacted. The hair on the back of my neck stood on end and my stomach was in knots.

"Oh my! I'm so sorry." The words escaped from my lips before I even had a chance to look up and realize I'd just walked right into the chest belonging to Caleb.

"Hey, Natasha. You should pay more attention where you're going. We keep running into each other like this."

Caleb's voice was teasing, but my heart was still pounding. The grip on my arm tightened slightly before I could pull it away from Caleb's grasp.

"Troy." The iciness in Caleb's voice was clear.

"Caleb." Troy's voice was rigid with tension. "I think you can let go of Natasha's arm."

The band of steel around my arm loosened and I was freed while I watched some unseen conversation going on between the two of them. "You guys know each other?" I asked.

"Yeah." Troy's reply was short.

"Wow, Natasha. I can't believe how quickly you get around. I didn't think you were that type of girl."

My head snapped back to Caleb. I was completely mortified. "What are you talking about? Troy is my boss. The whole office went out for dinner after work."

"Um hmm. Likely story. Well, you both enjoy yourselves." Caleb said with an edge to his voice.

Caleb's gaze pierced my heart. His eyes were cold, and I couldn't help but start to shiver. What had I done to him? I really needed to get the heck out of here right now. As Caleb walked toward the entry, I couldn't help but notice the slight shove of his shoulder he gave Troy as he walked past.

"Come on, let me walk you to the car. Sorry about that. Caleb can be kind of a dick," Troy commented.

"How do you guys know each other?" I asked still baffled by the side of Caleb I'd just witnessed. One I'd never seen before.

"It's a long story. Let's just say our families go way back."

"Oh, well, I have to say that until recently Caleb had been nothing but super helpful to me during school. But the last couple of weeks he's been like a totally different person."

Troy was walking beside me as we headed toward my car. I glanced up at his profile noticing his cheek muscle was twitching.

We finally reached my car and I unlocked it. Troy reached out and opened it for me and as I slid into the driver's seat his arm rested on the roof. "Be careful of Caleb. He's not what he seems to be."

"What do you mean?"

"Just like it sounds. I've known him almost my entire life. He plays a good game, but when he doesn't get what he wants, it doesn't always end well. I learned that the hard way."

"Okay. Thank you for the warning, I guess. I'll pay more attention when he's around."

"Have a good weekend Natasha. You did really well this week. I'm glad you have joined the team."

"Thanks Troy, and thanks for dinner, too. 'Night."

I started my car as Troy stepped away and firmly shut my door. Backing out of the parking stall, my thoughts were rambled. Troy's words tumbling through my mind over and over again. And the whole incident with Caleb threw me off balance. What in the world was going on with him? All year he'd been so nice, so helpful, but ever since I passed on the job at his family's office, it was like a light switch had been flipped. I didn't understand it. What was the big deal anyway?

The drive back to the dorm was quiet. The radio low in the background as my mind filtered back over the past week and I looked forward to a weekend to myself. With no homework and nothing that I had to do.

~ *Troy* ~

Natasha pulled her car out of the parking stall and I couldn't get her off my mind. There was an instinctive pull towards her and I wasn't sure exactly what it was. Yes, she was cute. Her dark long hair was such a contrast to her sparkling light blue eyes. Her cheeks were defined and tapered slightly down to her chin with a slight indent in the middle. Her makeup was light, more on the natural side, accenting her natural beauty.

But it was something more. It was a need to protect her. From what, I wasn't sure. Something was wrong, and I couldn't place my fingers on it, but it was eerie. Something that put all my senses on high alert.

Pulling my keys from my pocket I walked across the parking lot to my car for the quick drive home. Typically, on Friday nights I'd often hang out with the rest of the office, but tonight I just wasn't feeling it.

I hadn't seen Caleb in a long time, and I really didn't care to run into him again any time soon. Did I miss our friendship? Sometimes, yes. But that ended three years ago. My family would never be the same, and I would never forgive Caleb for his part in destroying it.

CHAPTER NINE

~ *Natasha* ~

The pounding on my dorm room door was driving me insane. *Come on!* It was Saturday morning! Who the heck was trying to get into my room? I knew it wasn't Justine. She had a key first off and she wasn't supposed to be back until tomorrow. Rolling out of my warm comfortable bed, I staggered to the door and opened it. I was tired, grumpy and just wanted to crawl back into my bed.

"SURPRISE!" both of my best friends, Mia and Bailey, yelled in unison. I was in shock, and denial, until I felt their warm strong arms wrapped around me.

"You look like crap," Mia said as she and Bailey entered my room.

"Well, hello to you too." I laughed. "I am still half asleep. What the hell are you guys doing up here?"

"Since you decided to bail on us this summer, we decided to come visit you for the weekend," Bailey explained.

Hugging each of them again, it was really good to have them here. I missed them. But my panic was bubbling just under the surface. My friends could read me like a book and I wasn't sure I wanted to tell them what had happened to me.

"Come on, get ready. I'm starving, and you're taking us out for breakfast. We need to celebrate this new job that you got." Mia stated as she plopped down on the chair at my desk.

"Alright, alright. Let me at least take a quick shower." I said laughing. It was good to see them. I didn't realize how much I'd missed them until they were standing right in front of me.

The small restaurant was bustling with activity. It wasn't anything elaborate, but the food was top notch and was constantly packed in the mornings. Both Bailey and Mia sat across from me chatting away. I was still in disbelief that they were sitting here and had flown all the way up to see me for the weekend.

A warm, gooey cinnamon roll sat in front of me lathered in frosting. It was my ultimate favorite, but I hadn't had much of an appetite lately. Pushing a piece around on my plate, I was startled when a napkin was tossed in my face.

"Hey, what was that for?" I asked as I playfully tossed it back at my friends across the booth from me.

"Um, we've asked you several questions and you're totally zoned out in another world. What is going on?" Mia asked.

"Come on. Tasha. Something is bothering you." Bailey stated quietly.

Both my friends rarely called me by my full name. Hearing my nickname made me feel at home, safe, secure, and comfortable. Bailey had always been the more quiet, calm one of us. Mia was by far the loudest of us, and never minced words. She told it just like she saw it.

"I'm fine. It was just a rough semester. My final project was intense. I didn't sleep much and then rolling right into my new job. I've had a lot going on."

"I've seen you stressed before; this is different. There's something else going on," Mia stated.

Placing my fork on the table, I looked at both of my friends sitting quietly and patiently across from me. This is exactly why I hadn't been ready to go home yet. I knew they would see right through me. We didn't have secrets between us, we'd all been through too much together and we could read each other so well. I knew with every bone in my body that I wasn't going to be able to make it through the day without telling them. They weren't going to let up.

"Okay, fine. Yes, there's something else going on, or actually something that happened, but I don't want to talk about it here, okay?"

Bailey and Mia gave each other a side glance, and I saw the silent message pass between them. At that moment, I knew that Mia hadn't been fooled when I talked to her the other day. She'd read me even through the phone.

"This is why you guys flew up here, huh?" I asked.

"Mia thought something was wrong when she talked to you the other day," Bailey answered.

"I barely said anything on the phone," I replied.

"I know, but it was how you said it, and what you didn't say. It's not like you to just switch up plans so quickly. And then when I talked to you, I could hear it in your voice. I knew something else was going on," Mia explained.

The tears were bubbling at the surface and I knew we needed to get out of here quickly. I refused to have a meltdown in the middle of the restaurant. I motioned the waitress over for our bill while Mia quickly grabbed it and tossed her card into the folder to pay.

Pulling out my wallet, I tossed cash onto the table to cover my portion of the bill. Mia waved me off, pushing it back toward me.

"No way. I've got it. You can get the next one," Mia stated as she handed the leather folder back to the waitress.

"Bailey, I thought you weren't coming back to Riverview until next week?" I asked.

"I'm not. I caught a flight from Vegas and met Mia at the airport. I wasn't working this weekend and when Mia called, we were able to get flights that landed within a couple of hours of each other."

"You guys are crazy you know. You didn't need to come all the way up here. It had to have cost a fortune for a last-minute flight."

"It's just money. You are more important, and we knew that you needed us, even though you were being stubborn and not saying anything," Mia replied.

I could feel the tears pooling and I quickly tried to brush them away before they spilled down my cheeks. "I don't know what I'm going to do without you guys."

"Sadly, I think you're stuck with us," Mia stated as the waitress brought back Mia's card and receipt.

The walk back to my car was silent as I could feel the comfort and support of my friends on each side of me. I tried to reign in my tears and figure out how I was going to tell them. I still had so many unanswered questions I didn't even know what to say.

A HEALING TOUCH

Sitting on my bed cross legged with both of my friends sitting across from me, I fumbled for the words. The tears were flowing, and it was so hard to get the story out. What I remembered, what I didn't remember, what the doctor had told me, my questions, my uncertainties, my fears.

My best friends sat there and cried with me, hugged me, and in the end, I did feel like part of the huge weight I'd been carrying for the past couple of weeks begin to lighten.

"I just don't know what to do," I stated. My eyes I'm sure were swollen and red from all the crying. "I have no idea who it was and every guy that comes up to me I look at them and wonder, was he the one? I hate it. I feel like I'm being watched and the deepest part of me stripped away and I'm so scared I'm never going to feel normal again."

"Oh Tasha, I'm so sorry." Bailey's arms were wrapped around me, holding me tight. "In time, things will slowly get better. I promise. And you've got both of us here anytime for support."

Bailey had been through so much in her own life. I knew she could relate. Her past was different, losing her entire family in a car accident while she was the only survivor. But that fear of wondering if life would ever move forward, I knew we now shared. Collin had come into her life and helped her move forward, healing, and putting the past behind her. It had taken time, and she had grown stronger. Today she was able to talk about her family without it bringing tears and nightmares.

"I know it's a different kind of pain and hurt, but falling thirty feet off a chair lift was no picnic either. But you were there for me too. You can get through this.

Whatever we can do to help you, you've got it, no questions asked," Mia added.

Mia was right. She'd almost died losing a massive amount of blood, damage to her liver, and having a kidney removed. But she powered through as stubborn and determined as she always was, refusing to let it stop her from living life.

"I'm glad you guys decided to come up. I've just been so stressed out and so unsure of myself and what to do. I didn't want to tell you guys. It's hard for me to even think about it. All I want to do is shove it into a deep dark compartment and lock it all away. Pretend it never happened. But then little things send me into a complete panic and I'm afraid I'm going to have a breakdown."

"If you found out who did it, would you press charges?" Mia asked

"Probably, but I don't think it's likely I'll ever know. I have no memories of what happened. Whoever it was used a condom, so there wasn't clear evidence. They kept everything, all my clothes and took all kinds of samples from me. Like under my fingernails. I don't know if there's any DNA evidence on any of that. Right now, it's all in a rape kit that the hospital collected.

"The scary part is because I don't know who it was. It could have been a complete stranger that I'll never run into again, or it could be someone I know, and that's what freaks me out so bad. Part of me wants to leave the area and go to a different school, so I'd never chance running into the person again. But then the stubborn part of me gets so angry that someone could cause me to want to run away from my scholarship and have that much control over my life. And that part is what makes me want to stand and fight, but I don't know if I'm strong enough."

"Tasha, you are a lot stronger than you think. Every day it will get a little better. And we're here, always. It doesn't matter day or night, any time you every need us you can always reach out to us. We may be separated by hundreds of miles right now, but we're only a text or call away." Bailey's voice was calming as her hand held mine tight, almost as if she was passing along some of her strength and sharing it with me.

I slid forward reaching for both of my friends in a tight hug, their arms wrapped tightly around me, and I cried. Crying harder even than I had the morning I'd stumbled back to the dorm.

Finally, releasing so much of the pent-up fear and emotions that I'd been shoving further and further into a black hole, where it could do nothing but eventually destroy me. Letting it out and leaning on my friends for support was refreshing.

A cleansing of my soul that I had needed more than I'd known. But they did, they knew me, knew me so well that even with a quick phone call that I had needed them without even uttering a word. Lifelong friends, a bond that I hoped we'd always have. Right now, they were my strength when I had none, my courage when all I wanted to do was to run away. I would get through this. I just needed to take it one day at a time.

CHAPTER TEN

~ *Natasha* ~

*M*onday morning came quick. My weekend with Bailey and Mia had been a blur of activity. After telling my best friends what had happened on Saturday, they'd urged me to file an official police report. Both of them had gone with me while I filled out all the paperwork and documented what had happened. One more step taken forward to get back control over my life.

Justine had gotten a chance to meet them both briefly Sunday night before I had dropped them off at the airport. Everyone had gotten along like they'd known each other forever. It was weird how sometimes people clicked like that, but I wasn't surprised considering how quickly Justine and I had bonded.

I'd been so exhausted I'd almost slept through my alarm. If it hadn't been for Justine shaking me awake, I probably would have slept the morning away and been late for work. Rushing through my shower and getting dressed, I felt more like myself than I had the past few weeks. Like a huge weight had been lifted from my shoulders.

After parking my car in the office parking lot, I had five minutes to spare. Even though the office was pretty relaxed, I didn't want to be late. I didn't see Kelsey's car in the parking lot yet so at least I wasn't the last one in this morning.

Camille's smiling face greeted me when I entered the lobby. "Good Morning, Natasha."

"Morning Camille."

Walking into the open work area, I realized that almost everyone from the office was in the conference room. The lights were dimmed, and construction photos were up on the LCD screen. The atmosphere radiating from the room was one of tension. Something must have gone wrong because no one sitting in there looked pleased.

Hurrying to my desk, I planned to stay out of the way and focus on what I needed to get done. I was reading through my emails when Kelsey plopped down in her chair with coffee in both hands.

"Oh, it's that kind of morning I see." I laughed at her.

"No, silly, one of these is for you. I hope I got it right. Iced caramel macchiato, upside down and extra caramel; right?" Kelsey stated as she handed me the cup on her left.

"Dang, you nailed it. How'd you remember that? I only ordered that once in front of you."

"I pick up things quickly," she smiled.

"Well, thank you very much. You have no idea how much I could use the caffeine this morning."

"I think it's going to be one of those days."

"Yeah, I kind of think you're right," I agreed.

The morning flew by. Kelsey and I worked quietly at our computers while the rest of the office was still tied up in the conference room. I had no idea how long they had been in there before I arrived, but it looked like they were finally wrapping things up as Evan and Jordan had already left the room. Thomas, Troy, and Alex were still inside.

Thomas and Troy had been drawing diagrams on the white board while they talked. I was really curious to know what was going on in there but wasn't comfortable enough to ask. Kelsey, who didn't seem to miss a beat, had picked up on my subtle glances towards the glass conference room.

"I'm pretty sure it's the office building they are discussing. They're working on getting all the framing issues fixed. They've been spending a lot of time trying to stay ahead of the issues and get them resolved so the project doesn't get delayed," Kelsey explained.

"Does everyone get involved like that on projects?" I asked.

"Not usually. It's typically only the project manager and then whoever is the architect of record. Troy does a lot too, but since he's not licensed yet, either Thomas or Jordan is the lead architect on projects."

"Are Evan and Alex taking their exams too?"

"I think Evan has taken a couple of them. I'm not sure about Alex, but neither seem to be in a hurry to finish them. At least not like Troy. He's been taking one almost every month. I think he's only got one or two left to go."

I noticed Troy leaving the conference room and heading straight towards Kelsey and myself. He looked tired and edgy.

"Morning Kelsey. Morning Natasha."

"Morning," both Kelsey and I said in unison.

"Natasha, were you able to get some construction shoes?"

"Yes, I have them in my car like Camille suggested."

"Okay, good. Go grab them. You're coming with me to the construction site. We'll leave here shortly. You'll need a hard hat too. There's extras in the break room."

"Okay. I'll be right back." Excitement bubbled through me. I was going to get to walk a real construction site. It would be my first. I was so glad my shoes had arrived. I'd had to order them online since I couldn't find any local that fit me.

Kelsey was grinning at me as I closed out of the file I'd been working on. "You lit up like it was Christmas."

"I'd been hoping I'd get to go out to a jobsite."

"Have fun! Make sure you use the bathroom before you go because the porta potties on the jobsites are seriously disgusting if you ever have to use one."

"Oh. Yeah, I guess I hadn't thought about that. Thanks for the heads up."

⌒⌒⌒

Troy was focused on the road in front of us. We'd taken the company truck that Thomas usually drove. Troy had given me his iPad that was open to the plans for the project and had quickly gone over the issues they were having onsite before we'd left the office. He'd told me to review the set of plans on the way so I would have a bit of background once we reached the site.

We'd been in the truck for almost twenty minutes. I looked at the address on the plans to see where we were headed. Running the location on my phone app it looked like we should be there shortly. The drive had been eerily quiet. I could tell that Troy was deep in thought. It was almost like I wasn't even in the truck with him.

Me on the other hand, was having a very hard time focusing on the plans I was scrolling through. My whole body felt electrified. I was conscious of every breath, of every sigh that Troy uttered. I finally couldn't take the silence anymore.

"Are you okay?" Geez, that was subtle. I wanted to kick myself. Couldn't have asked any other question, could I?

Troy's head snapped in my direction before quickly looking back to the road. "What?" he asked.

"Sorry, I mean I guess I don't know you very well yet. But you seem to be upset." I tried to justify my stupid question.

This time he smiled when he glanced toward me. "Don't be sorry. I should be the one apologizing. I rushed you out of the office without much explanation and then haven't said two words to you. Our morning started pretty early with text messages from the contractor that was urgent, and they needed a solution immediately. I thought you'd enjoy getting to walk the construction site."

"I am, I'm really excited and very appreciative that you're allowing me to tag along. I just didn't want to get in your way or be a bother."

"Natasha, trust me, you could never be a bother, and I am happy that you are coming along." Troy's smile lit a fire deep within me. I smiled back not knowing exactly how to respond to that. My cheeks, I'm sure had turned a deep crimson, as they felt like they were on fire.

⁓

The construction site was larger than I'd imagined. It was a three-story office building with two main wings that anchored a large open atrium. Visually seeing the building in three-dimensions from the plans I'd been looking through was a new experience.

Troy and I had been onsite for over an hour walking the building. He'd stop and show me different stages of the construction. With the multi stories they start on the first floor so it was in a different stage of completion than the third floor so I was able to see progression of work.

I had been introduced to the superintendent and several of the subcontractor's foremen. Everyone was nice and answered any question that I asked. I'd been a little worried that they'd think my questions were dumb. Before I knew it, we were back in the truck headed back to the office.

"So, what do you think?" Troy asked as we pulled out of the dirt lot onto the adjacent street. His eyes catching mine as he turned to look my direction.

"It's so much bigger in person than how I visualized it in my head."

"The more experience you have, the more you'll anticipate issues and how the project goes together. We always take a lot of photos when we go onsite. We have to document the progress. We can also go back to those photos later once walls and floors are covered up if we need to reference utilities or infrastructure. I saw you were taking photos too. It's always a good thing to keep folders of the images at the different stages so you can keep them organized for later. I'll show you how we write up our job site observation report when we get back to the office. Photos are always a part of that report."

"Thanks again for bringing me today. I also understand now why we have to wear protective shoes. I think I stepped on at least three screws while walking around."

"If you'd been wearing regular shoes those screws would have likely been embedded into your feet and that wouldn't have been fun. When they are installing the steel stud framing that's typically when the site is the messiest. It's really hard to keep the framers on task and cleaning up after themselves," Troy explained.

"Do you think there will be more problems with the framing?" I asked.

"Hopefully not. The general contractor had enough, and they fired the previous framing sub. The framers onsite today are a new crew. That's one reason why it was important for us to come out and review everything."

Flipping through the photos I'd taken on my phone, I was starting to realize that not only had I taken a ton of the site, but there were a lot of them that Troy was in. When I was taking them, I hadn't realized that he had been in so many of the shots. Looking through them all I was a little embarrassed, my subconscious was obviously focused on other things. I'd need to delete some of these before I showed anyone. I didn't want anyone getting the wrong idea.

A HEALING TOUCH

A huge explosion ripped through the truck. I looked up in alarm at the road as I heard Troy curse under his breath. "What was that?" I asked.

"I'm pretty sure it's a tire," Troy stated.

"A tire? What happened to the tire?" I could feel and hear the rumble through the truck. Troy pulled along the shoulder of the country road we were currently on. Literally out in the middle of nowhere.

"Feels and sounds like we've got a flat. I probably drove over some nails or screws in the construction lot. They are supposed to sweep for metal daily but that doesn't always happen, and it doesn't always pick them all up."

Troy flipped on his hazard lights as he put the truck in park. "Stay in the truck, I'll see how bad it is. I should be able to get the spare on. It'll be fine." He smiled as he shut the door.

My phone had one little bar for signal. I'm sure it wasn't a big deal. These things happened. Troy didn't seem to be worried. I watched him as he walked around the truck and stopped to inspect the rear passenger tire. I felt dumb just sitting in the truck waiting so I jumped out of the truck and walked over to him.

"Well at least the rim isn't hurt, but the tire is shredded. It shouldn't have fallen apart that quickly. I stopped as soon as I heard it."

"What can I do to help?"

"The jack, wrench, and bars are under the rear passenger seat. Flip up the seat and pull them out. I'll get the spare out."

Troy went to the back of the truck while I fumbled with the seat, trying to lift it up. It couldn't be that difficult. I was getting frustrated and refused to tell him I was so incompetent that I couldn't even get the tools out. Finally, the seat flipped up, almost knocking me off balance.

The jack and tools were right there where he said they'd be under the seat. I pulled them out and walked to the back of the truck. Troy took the two bars from my hands and connected them. I watched in fascination as he inserted them into a small hole in the tailgate and the spare tire slowly lowered down to the ground from under the truck.

"Huh, wow, I guess I never thought about how you'd get that thing out," I stated

Troy looked up from where he was pulling the tire out from under the truck. "Well, ideally, you'd never have to be in a situation where you'd actually have to use it. You can always search it online, too. It'll show videos on how to release it."

"Yeah, but if you don't have any signal for your phone that's not going to help." I replied.

"Then you old school it, and pull the book out." Troy smiled as he rolled the tire over to the flat one.

As I watched Troy start to release the flat tire, the breeze began to pick up and a loud clap of thunder shattered the quiet.

"You've got to be kidding me," I stated. "I don't remember seeing rain in the weather for this week."

"Well, hopefully it's just threatening, and we can get this done quickly." Troy started working even faster to get the tire loose.

My lightweight sweater was no match for the wind and the very large drops of water that was starting to fall from the sky. I shivered as I stood next to Troy, handing him the jack now that the tire was loose.

"You don't have to stand out here. You can stay in the cab. No sense in both of us getting soaked." Troy said as he took the jack.

"I'm okay. I'm not leaving you out here. You wouldn't happen to have an umbrella in the truck, would you?"

"Maybe. I don't remember seeing one though, but it's worth checking."

I searched through the backseat and the front, checking all the compartments. The truck was immaculate, but no umbrella.

"No luck." I said as I came back to where Troy was repositioning the jack. The clouds had darkened quickly and let loose. Instantly, we were both drenched.

"So much for threatening." I laughed.

Troy chuckled as he finally pulled the tire off and slid the spare in its place.

"I do love the smell when it rains though. We don't get rain much in Riverview. I love how everything gets washed clean and it's like a fresh start."

Troy looked up at me, his eyes searching mine. It was like he could see through me. It made me nervous and very unsettled. How could a glance get to me that intensely?

He didn't say anything but just turned back to his task and finally tightened the last lug nut. Double checking that they were all secure, he rolled the damaged tire to the tailgate.

"Toss the tools in the back floorboard for now and get out of the rain. I just need to throw the tire into the bed and we can get out of here."

I picked up the jack with the other tools, and was hurrying to open the back passenger door when my feet lost their footing on the slick dirt. I fell and landed with a thud on the now muddy shoulder. Mud splashed all over me and up onto the truck.

"Natasha!" Troy yelled as he ran over to me. "Are you okay?"

With my hands holding the tools I had nothing to break my fall. I landed hard on my side. My sweater had slid up, and it felt like I'd scraped my side. I was more stunned than I think I was hurt. More than anything else though, I was embarrassed. I felt like a clumsy idiot.

"I'm fine."

"Here, let me help you up."

Troy grabbed the tools from my hands, and with his other hand pulled me upright. When I finally looked up, I was practically against his chest. I could feel the warmth from his body. His hand still held mine, holding me steady on my feet.

"You sure you're not hurt anywhere?" He asked, concern evident as he studied me.

I was slightly dizzy but wasn't sure if it was from the fall or the proximity to which I was currently standing next to Troy. The rain pelted down on us and in that moment, I honestly didn't care that I was soaking wet.

Troy released my hand as his finger reached up to my face and brushed my nose and my cheek. "You had mud splattered on your face. Are you okay?"

I nodded my head yes. My nerves were rattled and the next thing I knew I was laughing. First it started as a slight giggle and then before I could stop it, I was laughing almost hysterically.

"I'm sorry, it's just something that happens to me sometimes when I'm stressed. I'll start laughing."

Troy smiled. "You have a cute laugh. You should laugh more often. Now, as long as you're sure you're okay, let's get out of here before something else happens."

Troy stepped in front of me and opened the passenger door. I climbed in, and felt his hand slightly on my back as I slid into the front seat and pulled the door shut. Without Troy's heat against me, my body chilled quickly.

The passenger back door opened, and he tossed the tools inside. I watched in the side mirror as he returned to the rear of the truck and shut the tailgate, and then sprinted back to the driver's side. He slid behind the wheel and started the truck. Leaning in the backseat he grabbed a sweatshirt and handed it to me.

"I always toss an extra sweatshirt in the car. You never know when you might need one."

"Thank you." Sliding the sweatshirt over my head, I breathed in deeply, smelling Troy's cologne. I wasn't sure exactly what it was, but I liked it. It was a light, clean, somewhat woodsy, maybe even a hint of citrus smell. I couldn't quite figure it out. I snuggled into the warmth of the thick sweatshirt and let the scent wrap around me.

"Let's get the heat on and you warmed up. I think your first trip to a construction site will be one you'll never forget." He laughed as he maneuvered the truck back onto the road.

CHAPTER ELEVEN

~ *Natasha* ~

Summer was almost over. My internship would be complete in one week and I was sad that it would be coming to an end. I had loved every minute of every day I'd spent in the DeLuca Architecture office.

I was hoping that there was a way I could stay. I loved working with everyone in the office. It was like an extended family. I'd felt comfortable immediately and had learned so much in the few short weeks I'd been there. I knew my fall term would be packed with classes and studio with very little spare time, but even if I could work a couple days a week that would be awesome.

I'd miss the weekly Friday night dinners with everyone as well. Kelsey had become a close friend, and I enjoyed working with her. But if I was completely honest with myself; not being able to see Troy every day was likely going to be the most difficult. There was a pull toward him I couldn't deny anymore, but I also wasn't going to jeopardize my chance to continue to work there in the future. Besides, I was sure he only saw me as another co-worker and nothing more.

Each day that passed I grew stronger, and a felt like a little more of myself return. I still had my moments of panic and wanting to run, but I knew I really had come a long way since Bailey and Mia had surprised me with their visit at the beginning of the summer. They checked on me often, as I knew they would. Their concern and being there for me was what I had needed. We'd been there for each other for years and I knew we'd always have a special bond, no matter how far apart we were.

Throughout the summer Justine had been my shadow whenever I went out. I knew that having her strong presence had also helped me start my healing. I still struggled with anyone who touched me though. I hoped that eventually I'd get to a point where I wouldn't go into a panic attack anytime a stranger brushed up against me.

It was Friday and the afternoon was quickly slipping away. I was looking forward to the weekly dinner in a few hours. Kelsey continued to try to get me out on the dance floor every week but something kept holding me back. I knew that I wasn't ready for that yet and wasn't going to push my luck.

Since running into Caleb the night at the restaurant, I hadn't seen him all summer. I didn't know if I was sad or relieved. I'd seen a side of him that I hadn't seen the entire year of him helping me in the studio. That little bit of temper that I'd seen frightened me to my core and made me question my ability to read people.

The location of my desk against Kelsey's gave me a perfect view into Troy's office. I often found myself distracted watching him as he worked. He was patient, and quiet, but fiercely dedicated to his work. He spent time explaining why he made changes or markups on our plans which I appreciated. I felt like I was actually learning things instead of just mindlessly drafting plans.

I couldn't quite figure him out. He almost always attended the office Friday night dinners, but during the rest of the week he was more distant than the rest of the people who worked in the office.

Kelsey's banter towards him was significantly different than how everyone else talked to him. It was pretty obvious they were good friends, and I wondered how and why they had never dated. They seemed to click really well. But even as the thought crossed my mind, I pushed it away. It stirred feelings in me that I didn't want to deal with. Feelings that had continued to grow over the last few weeks.

There was something about Troy that called to me. Something I couldn't put my finger on. It was like a weighted blanket that had been wrapped around me, soothing away and damping the pain. Even though our conversations were never more than work related there was something more, something deeper crackling under the surface.

A connection that I couldn't explain. Almost felt like he had this sense of knowing what I had been through even though I'd never uttered a word to him about it or to anyone in the office. It was impossible to put into words the feelings that raced through me.

Movement in Troy's office caught my attention as he stood up from his desk. His gaze directed at me. With a slight motion of his hand, I knew he wanted me to come into his office. As I pushed back my chair to see what he wanted, he sat back down behind his computer and tapped something out on his keyboard.

When I reached the open door of his office I stood and waited for him to finish whatever he was typing. He looked up briefly while his fingers continued to type.

A HEALING TOUCH

"Have a seat Natasha. I'm almost done."

I pulled the guest chair back, and slid silently in the chair, watching him as he worked. He wore a white long-sleeved button-down shirt today tucked into jeans. He had the sleeves rolled up almost three quarters. He always looked classy and casual at the same time.

Troy's eyes shifted in color. I couldn't quite figure out if they were more gray or more green as they seemed to change even during the day. It depended on the light, what he was wearing, the weather; it was like nothing I'd ever really seen before.

His hair was slightly tousled and I knew that was because he'd been running his fingers through it earlier when he had been on a phone call. Whoever he'd been talking to he had been irritated with because his voice had risen on several occasions during the call.

Kelsey had been right about his moods. While most of the time he was pretty easy going, there were days when he was super moody and snappy. Kelsey would give me that look, and I knew it was best to stay clear of his office. While he'd never snapped at me. I'd seen several others get the brunt of it and I had no desire to be at the receiving end of one of those conversations.

During the entire summer, I'd never seen Troy with a date. No one came to the office to see him for lunch, or to the Friday office dinners. Kelsey had said he was focused on work, but there had to be someone out there. He was just too hot not to have women vying for his attention. Maybe he was gay. He didn't keep pictures on his desk, so there were no answers there. I'm sure Kelsey would know, but I'd never had the guts to ask her.

The clicking on the keyboard stopped, and my eyes snapped back to Troy's face. His steady gaze was direct, and I could feel heat flush instantly across my face. I wanted to die right there while I sat in the chair.

I hoped he had no idea what thoughts had been playing through my head, or the visual inspection I'd just given him. I knew I could be an open book sometimes, even though I worked hard to conceal my emotions. I hated having everyone be able to read me.

"School is starting back up for you in a couple of week. How have you enjoyed your internship this summer?"

"I've loved it. I've learned so much. Everyone has been so helpful and supportive. I was actually kind of hoping that you might have something part time that might work with my schedule when I go back to school."

"I'm glad you feel that way. You've been an asset to the company, and I brought you in here to see if you might want to stay on. I know balancing work and school can be difficult, but if you're willing and up for the challenge, then the job is yours. School is the most important though, so you need to keep us updated if there are times when you need to be focused on your school projects. We've all been there. We understand."

"I don't know what to say. Honestly. I was really starting to dread next week thinking that my internship would be over."

"Everyone that has worked with you has been very impressed with how quickly you've picked up on things. You listen, you work hard, and everyone likes you too." Troy smiled as he sat back in his chair.

"I'm signed up for my classes already. Should I just give you my open available time slots during the week?"

"That would be great. You can email them over and we'll get it figured out."

"Thank you, Troy. I'm so grateful for this opportunity."

"You are very welcome. You deserve it Natasha. You have a natural talent. You're going to do well in this field. Go finish what you were working on. The day's almost over and we'll all celebrate tonight at dinner."

I smiled. I was starting to fit in, and become a part of this amazing team and it was the best feeling ever. "Sounds like fun. I'm looking forward to it."

~ *Troy* ~

Our regular table for dinner was full tonight. Even my dad and mom had joined us, in celebration of bringing Natasha onboard as a regular employee and not just as a temporary summer intern.

My dad had been just as impressed with her work as I had. She had worked hard all summer and she deserved the opportunity. We'd had interns over the years that just never cut it, but Natasha was a keeper.

I'd noticed a change in her over the weeks too. She was slowly coming out of her shell. She was reserved and quiet, but I could see that she was starting to feel comfortable around the team.

There were still moments though when I could sense something was off. I still hadn't been able to put my finger on it, but it was there, just bubbling under the surface.

I kept her working on my projects. I found myself enjoying spending time with her. Reviewing drawings, explaining different processes, or design options. Jordan had asked to have her help him on one of his projects and immediately a wave of jealously had crept over me. I had come up with an excuse on why he should use Kelsey instead. Jordan had given me a look like he knew I was pulling at straws, but he never questioned me. He just gave me a slight smile and walked away.

He had been with our company for over ten years, and was the other licensed architect on staff. He was easygoing and very detailed. My dad had trained him and took him under his wing right after school. He'd spent many dinners at our house and was almost like an older brother to me. I knew he saw right through me but I didn't care.

Natasha's arm brushed mine slightly as she was seated to my left. Every week we sat in these same seats and talked. Sometimes the table was packed like it was tonight and other nights there were only a few of us.

Something about her was still strangely familiar and I couldn't put my finger on it. With her growing up in Southern California, I knew it wasn't that we'd crossed paths in the past, but something was there, just lingering beyond my grasp.

Natasha had spent most of dinner blushing as everyone took a turn welcoming her to the company and complimenting her on something that they felt that she did really well.

The DJ in the corner had finished setting up and the lights in our section of the restaurant had dimmed as dance music began to filter across the space. Natasha never stayed when the dancing started. She would always find an excuse on why she had to leave. Tonight,

Kelsey was being even more persuasive, trying to get her out on the floor.

Alex, his fiancé Alyssa, Evan, and his wife Jennifer were already out on the floor as well as Jordan and his wife Lisa. It wasn't often that Jordan and Lisa made it out, but tonight they were enjoying the night without their kids.

"Come on Natasha. Just one dance," Kelsey begged.

"I'm just not much into dancing anymore."

"What do you mean anymore?" I asked

"I mean, I'm just not a very good dancer," Natasha replied.

"I think you're a good dancer. I saw you that night a couple months ago at the beginning of the summer when you were with your roommate."

"Oh, um, it's just not usually my thing."

"Please Natasha, it will be fun. We're celebrating and you haven't stayed after dinner for dancing at all this summer. It's Friday night. It's your last week before you get back to your full class load at school. It's time for some fun," Kelsey argued.

I watched the hesitation flicker across Natasha's face. She was clearly struggling with something more than dancing. But then she sighed.

"Alright, alright, you win Kelsey. Okay, fine. One dance, one, but then I've got to go." Natasha smiled slightly, and Kelsey snagged her arm and pulled her quickly to the dance floor, laughing and smiling the entire time.

The two reached the dance floor where the rest of our group was already swaying to the music. Natasha was uncomfortable. I could feel it even across the room.

Her smile was tight, her movements stiff, but after a bit I could see her starting to relax and enjoy herself.

"Well, I think your mom and I are going to head out. Why don't you go join those girls? No sense in them dancing by themselves." My dad chuckled as he stood and pulled my mom's chair out for her.

Pushing back my chair, I stood, leaning over and giving my mom a quick hug before she left.

"She's really cute Troy. I've seen how you watch her. I'm not sure why you haven't asked her out already." My mom whispered in my ear as she hugged me back.

"Is it really that obvious?" I asked as I pulled away and looked at my mom.

"I know you Troy. I don't think it's noticeable to anyone else. Go. Go dance, have fun. I'll talk to you later."

"Bye Mom" I smiled. "Dad, I'll talk to you later."

~ *Natasha* ~

My heart was still pounding. I swore my chest was probably moving up and down with each beat. The urge to run from the dance floor was so strong, the exit door calling my name.

I was struggling to get my breathing under control and I couldn't understand what it was about dancing and the music that kept sending me into a panic. I was pretty sure I hadn't been dancing the night at the party when my whole world shifted, but maybe I had gone back in and danced. I really didn't know.

A HEALING TOUCH

I couldn't remember and I still didn't know if that was a blessing or a curse. I hated not knowing. Not knowing if I would run into the person that had taken away a part of me I'd never get back. Knowing that some other girl could fall victim to the same thing.

Kelsey swayed to the music, enjoying herself. I tried to smile and relax but I was really struggling. I knew I looked as awkward as I felt. I hated that. I hated that one person could strip from me my self-confidence, my security, my innocence. I wanted myself back.

Some days were easier, but some days were so hard I didn't know how I was going to make it through. The reality was thinking about the what ifs wasn't going to help me. I knew that deep down, but it didn't make it any easier for me.

I felt his presence before I saw him. The last few weeks I'd tried to ignore it. I couldn't deal with any more emotions right now, but there was something about Troy that kept pulling me toward him. His presence calmed me.

When every other thought and feeling that I had pushed me to run, there was this small part of me that was drawn to him. A gravitational pull. It was the only time in the past few months when I felt a little bit of my old self peek out.

Kelsey was in her element, bouncing between our coworkers and their significant others. Laughing and singing to each song. She was so carefree and outgoing. I longed to be able to just let go and be more like her.

I felt the light brush of Troy's hand as it grazed my hip. In that second, goosebumps traveled across my body. Emotions so strong, like nothing I'd ever felt before flooded my veins. His eyes studied mine. His hand was still lightly resting on my hip. That slight connection between us about unraveled me. Every nerve ending on full alert.

"Relax, it's okay," he whispered.

The fact that he knew I was freaking out almost pushed me out the door. Was it that obvious? Probably. The fear that raced through me was starting to slow down though. I'm sure I looked like a deer trapped in headlights with nowhere to run.

One breath at a time it was all I could do. His light touch on both my hips now seemed to ground me. I tried to shut everything else out around me. I didn't want to need anyone.

A part of me knew that I needed to let go and accept help in whatever form it took, and right now it was in the handsome presence of Troy. I didn't know why or how, but I needed that calm. I needed that strength.

My body slightly relaxed, the stiffness easing as I focused on him. How his body moved in rhythm to mine. Carefully, and hesitantly, my arms found their place loosely on his shoulder. My fingers interlocked behind his neck. My body shifting closer to his as we moved to the music.

Surprisingly, I no longer felt awkward. It felt like we'd danced a lifetime together and I didn't understand it. Being so close, I studied his eyes as they never left mine. For the first time, I realized there was a light amber ring that circled his pupil giving them much more of a green appearance tonight.

"You okay?" he asked

"Yeah."

His smile lit up his face. The light scruff of a day's growth, made him even more attractive. His grip on my hips increased just slightly, holding me to him, but not confining me. Song after song, we danced. It was the first time in months that I pushed everything away and had fun.

The rest of our group had already called it a night. Kelsey had made some new friends and was still there dancing alongside of us. Over Troy's shoulder, I caught Kelsey's smile and a thumbs up, causing me to laugh.

"What's so funny?" Troy asked

"Nothing, just Kelsey," I replied quickly

Troy turned his head to look back at Kelsey. She just shrugged her shoulders, making me laugh even harder.

"I like hearing you laugh. You should do it more often. I haven't heard you laugh like that since the day we had that flat tire."

I wasn't sure there was any way my cheeks could get redder, but they were on fire now with his compliment. "Um, thanks. There hasn't been much to laugh at lately."

"Well, I guess we'll have to work on that." He said with a smile that melted my heart.

It was well past one in the morning as the three of us finally left the restaurant. We walked Kelsey to her car. As she opened the door, she reached around and hugged me tight.

"Thanks for staying tonight and I'm so glad you aren't leaving us. I knew you were a good dancer too." Her voice dropped to a whisper as she leaned into my ear. "And you both make a cute couple." She chuckled as she slid into her car. "'Night guys!"

She put her car in reverse, and we started to walk to my car. Troy was in step beside me. His hand rested lightly at the small of my back as we walked. I liked how it felt. It was crazy how one small touch could make me feel protected and safe. Especially after weeks of isolation where fear and panic at every corner haunted me.

We reached my car and I unlocked it. Troy opened the driver door and stepped aside to let me in. I stopped and stood just inside the protection of my open door.

Troy stood on the other side with his arms resting on the top of the door frame. His fingers lightly brushed a loose strand of my dark, long hair behind my ear. His touch lingered there, then his fingers gently traced my jaw, lifting my chin slightly upward.

Suddenly the darkness crept into my brain. Immediately clouding my thoughts and within seconds my pulse was beating rapidly. My heart slamming inside my chest.

Pulling quickly away, I slid into my car. "I'm sorry, I've got to go."

I focused on getting my car started and backing up. Shutting out the confused expression on Troy's face as he stood there in the beam of my headlights, watching me drive away. He probably thought I was crazy, but right now I had to get as far away as possible.

The darkness that I'd been working so hard to push away was smothering me, choking me, pushing away what security and comfort I'd started to regain out of my grasp.

I felt myself slipping away like I was detached from my body and only watching it from afar go through the necessary movements to maneuver my car through the dark streets, while the shadows chased me.

A HEALING TOUCH

~ *Troy* ~

The light from Natasha's headlights slightly blinded me as I watched her pull away. It was like she couldn't get away from me fast enough. The change in her was as quick as flipping a light switch.

I replayed the last few minutes back in my head trying to figure out exactly what had caused such panic. I had seen it as it washed over her the moment my fingers touched her chin. In that second, she shut down. The carefree girl that had just danced with me had vanished.

A sickening feeling overwhelmed me. I was beginning to feel like I was reliving the past. The emotions, the reactions, the fear that I'd seen in Natasha, I'd seen before.

My heart broke for Natasha. I didn't know the details, and I didn't know if she would ever trust me enough to confide in me, but my gut was telling me that something very bad had happened to her.

This time though I vowed I wouldn't stand aside and let the darkness overtake her. I'd been in this place before and hadn't taken enough steps to help. I wouldn't make that same mistake again.

CHAPTER TWELVE

~ *Natasha* ~

As quietly as I could, I turned the key, and unlocked the door to my dorm room. It was late and I knew Justine would likely be asleep. But the light was still on as I entered the room. Justine was propped up in her bed reading on her iPad.

"You're out late." She said as she put the iPad on the bed next to her.

"Yeah, I stayed for a bit after our weekly dinner. We were celebrating me getting hired."

"Natasha! That's awesome. I'm so excited for you! That's what you'd been wanting right?"

"It is. I had really been dreading having to say goodbye to everyone."

Justine watched me as I set my purse and keys down. I could feel her stare as I grabbed my sleep shorts and top.

"What?" I asked.

"Something's not right. What else happened?"

"Nothing. I stayed after. Alex's fiancé was there and Evan's wife was there tonight too, even Jordan and his wife Lisa were there. Everyone danced for a bit. That's it."

"You danced too?"

"Yeah, it was fine."

"Natasha, come on, you don't seem fine. What happened? You can talk to me. I'm here for you. I'm glad you stayed. You need to do those types of things."

I sat cross-legged on my bed with my pjs in my hands. Justine got up from her bed and sat in front of me. Her deep brown eyes searching mine. She reminded me so much of Mia. They could have been sisters from their appearance but also their personalities.

"I don't know Justine. I really don't know." I said as I stared down into my lap. My pjs were now scrunched into a ball.

"Did someone say something? Or do something?" Justine asked carefully. Her hands covered mine.

"No, I'm not really sure what happened. Kelsey had been begging and begging for me to come dance with her like she does every week. I finally gave in. At first when I was out there with her, I just wanted to run for the exit.

"I finally started to relax a little bit. I had only planned to stay for one song, maybe two, just enough to pacify Kelsey. But then Troy joined all of us out on the dance floor. I've never stayed around for the dancing before so I really don't know if it's something they do often.

"All summer though Troy always left when I did so I don't think he ever went back. But the next thing I know is that I was dancing with Troy.

"Not just next to him, but I had my arms around his neck. His hands were on my hips. And I didn't feel scared. I didn't want to run. For the first time in months, I felt a little bit like my old self."

"That's a good thing Natasha. So why are you so upset about it?"

"Because when he walked me to my car right before I left, I freaked out."

"What do you mean 'freaked out'?"

"I freaked out. He opened my door for me and was standing there. He reached over and tucked a piece of my hair behind my ear. Then his fingers traced my jaw, and the minute he reached my chin and slightly tilted it, I just lost it.

"The darkness slammed into me. Shut me down completely. I jumped into my car and sped away. He's going to think I'm a nutcase Justine. And he won't be wrong. I am. There was no rational reason why I should have panicked at that moment."

"You are not a nutcase. Give yourself a break. It's only been a few weeks since everything happened. You've not gone to any counseling. You've been trying to deal with everything on your own. It's going to take some time."

"But I don't want it to take time. I want myself back. Now. I don't want to go talk to anyone. What am I going to say? I have no idea what even happened to me to even know how to deal with it. Most of that night is completely missing from my memory. If I can only make the rest of it disappear."

"I'm sorry love, I really am. But trying to make it disappear isn't going to help you. I've told you before I will go with you. Or even just take you to see someone. They can help you work through it and help you move forward."

"I'm not ready Justine. I can't talk to some stranger about what happened."

"Okay. I'm not going to push. But I'm here, and when you are ready, I'll still be here. So are Bailey and Mia. They flew all the way up here to make sure you were okay. We're all here for you Natasha. Whatever you need."

"Thanks. Really. I do appreciate it. And I couldn't have made it through this past summer without you."

"Troy is probably a little confused, but I'm sure everything is going to be okay. He doesn't seem like the type to be rattled easily. Speaking of Troy, what are your feelings toward him?"

"I don't know. I really don't. I'm so confused. One minute I feel safe and secure with him. The next minute, I'm running as far away as I can. I really like working with him. I've learned so much, but it's not just work. There's something else about him, something more that pulls me in. But there's a distance there too. I sense a wall around him, protecting him from something, and I'm not sure what."

"Maybe he's been hurt in the past. Most people do have some sort of wall around them. We all have some sort of battle wounds."

"I guess. I just don't know. I'm so confused."

"That's to be expected. All you can do is take one day at a time."

I leaned over and hugged my friend. I was really lucky to have her. Her support and understanding had been unwavering and I would never forget that.

———

I watched Natasha laugh while she danced and I burned with anger. Hands that weren't mine held her hip. Her arms wrapped around someone else's shoulders. But then I calmed when I realized that no matter what, I'd been there first. I'd been the first one to touch her, and no one would ever be able to take that away.

She was mine. She just didn't realize it yet. I had already claimed her, and I wasn't going to let someone else step in and take her away from me. She would be mine again.

CHAPTER THIRTEEN

~ *Natasha* ~

Silence had not been my friend lately. When I was busy things were easier to push away. When it was silent, my thoughts would drift into places that I didn't want to dwell on. I often wondered if it was my subconscious trying to force me to deal with the pain that I was trying so hard to avoid.

It was still early. The sun hadn't even started to break through the blinds. I'd slept horribly through the night. Well, actually I'd slept like crap all weekend if I was being honest with myself.

Friday night replayed in my head over and over again, and I was trying to figure out what had triggered my panic. Nothing made sense. I had no answers, and I didn't know what I was going to say to Troy when I saw him this morning.

So many times, during the weekend I'd typed out a text to send him to say I was sorry. But every time, I deleted it before I could send it. Everything I'd typed sounded so lame and ultimately, I think the worst part of it all was that I was embarrassed. Horrified actually, that I'd completely lost it in front of him for no good reason.

Rolling over, I decided I'd laid here long enough. I knew I wasn't going back to bed so I might as well get up and get ready for work.

～～～

The morning slipped by quickly. I had been so focused on my drawings that I hadn't even realized it was almost lunch. Movement in Troy's office caught my attention and I realized he'd just walked in. The door to his office closed behind him as he walked to his desk.

"Wow, I can't believe he actually came in today," Kelsey stated.

"Why?" I asked. I wasn't aware of any jobsite meetings today, but you never knew those would often just pop up spur of the moment.

"None of the family usually come in on this day. Or at least not since I've worked here."

"What's so significant about today?"

"You didn't know?"

"Know what?"

"Three years ago, Troy's sister, Talise, passed away. They say she overdosed on sleeping pills."

"Oh my God. I had no idea. I didn't even know he had a sister."

"Yeah, she was a few years younger than Troy. It was just before she was getting ready to start her freshman year in college. No one really knows why, or if they do no one has ever said anything. Troy was the one that found her unresponsive in her room. It was horrible. He took it really hard."

"I can't even imagine."

"Troy and I were just getting ready to start our third year of architectural school. School hadn't started yet for the quarter. Troy was working here in the office. I don't know all the particulars just the little bit that he told me.

"He'd forgotten something at home and ran home during his lunch break. Their dog was barking in Talise's room when Troy came home. Talise's door was open, and he found her curled up on her bed unconscious. She was still alive. Troy called 911, but by the time they got her to the hospital, she was gone, and they weren't able to bring her back.

"Talise had always been fun, and had a super bubbly personality. She had lots of friends and a bright future. She was an amazing artist. She loved the more creative side of architecture. The renderings of projects and model building.

"She worked on and off in the office during the summers and her breaks while she was in high school. That summer, she was a different person. Super withdrawn. He has always said he felt like he should have been able to do something to save her," Kelsey explained.

"One of my best friends back home lost her entire family in a car accident while we were in high school. She was the only one that survived. It really messed her up for a long time. She didn't understand how she could have survived when the rest of her family didn't. There's always some sort of guilt when there's a family loss like that."

"I'm still in a little shock that he even came in today. Maybe it's getting easier for them now that more time has passed. I'm really not sure. He doesn't talk about it."

"It's probably not something that is easy to talk about. I know with my friend, Bailey, she would rarely talk about her family. She had constant nightmares after the accident. It took her quite a long time to heal. I think part of her will never be fully healed, but she's learning to forgive herself and let herself move on with her life."

"Man, what time is it? I'm starving. Did you want to go grab lunch with me?" Kelsey asked.

"You're always starving," I said, laughing.

"Yeah, well, food and I have this special relationship going." Kelsey chuckled as she grabbed her purse.

"I'm good. I actually brought my lunch today. I'll just grab it from the fridge."

"Okay, well I'll be back. If you change your mind and want me to bring you something just text me."

Sitting at my computer screen, I was staring at the enlarged bathroom plan I was detailing, running through everything Kelsey had just told me. I couldn't help glancing over to Troy's office. He seemed pretty subdued. He never closed his office door. He moved closer to his desk. His elbows were bent. His fingers moving back and forth across his temples as he held his head in his hands. He looked miserable and my heart broke.

I'm not sure what possessed me, but the next thing I knew, I had gotten up and was standing in front of his closed glass door. I wondered, do I push it open? Do I knock? What the hell was I even doing?

He obviously wanted to be alone if he'd shut his door. But I couldn't turn away. I could feel his pain, and while I was trying to deal with my own issues, I couldn't walk away.

A HEALING TOUCH

I finally gently tapped on the glass door. Troy's head snapped up. I could see dark shadows under his eyes. After a long pause, he waved me in. I pushed down on the lever handle, and let the glass door close silently behind me. I quietly sat in the chair in front of his desk. I wondered what in the world was I going to even say to him now that I was sitting here in front of him. Maybe this was a bad idea.

~ *Troy* ~

I hated this day. Every year I tried to ignore it. Every year I thought it would be easier. But, it wasn't. Everyone always told me, '*time heals the hurt. It will get easier.*' I was beginning to think everyone was full of crap because it wasn't.

Every year I retraced my steps, wondering what I could have done different to have gotten to Talise earlier. To have seen how much she was hurting. To have paid more attention to her in those last weeks. I knew something was up with her. I knew it. But I was busy, and I chalked her moodiness up to just typical teenager drama.

I had tried to pin point the change in her. What went wrong. I had my suspicions, but no evidence. She had ripped several pages out of her journal that we found days after she had died.

So far, we'd never found those missing pages. She had probably thrown them away. They might have given us some sort of insight to what had happened. But now, we just had emptiness. No closure, and so many questions left unanswered.

I knew things had gone wrong with her boyfriend, but she never told me what. When I had confronted him after she had died, he'd just brushed me off. Saying she had just flipped out one night and didn't want anything to do with him anymore.

Every time I saw him around town it made me sick. I wanted to punch him if to just let go of some of the frustration that I continued to deal with. What could have gone so wrong in her life that she'd felt that it wasn't worth living anymore? I couldn't understand. Things always got better. Even when things were bad, there was always a light at the end of the tunnel. She had so much to live for.

My parents had already visited the cemetery, but I hadn't been able to go out there yet today. Part of me wondered what the hell I was even doing sitting in my office right now. I really was in no frame of mind to be working. I'd barely slept last night, and I was cranky. It wasn't a good combination.

I held my head in my hands, trying to rub away the headache that was rapidly coming on. The tapping on my office door snapped me out of my stew. I was about to yell at whoever was standing at my door to go away. I mean, seriously, I had shut the door for a reason. Most everyone knew to stay out if I had the door shut, since I usually never shut my door.

When I looked up into Natasha's clear blue eyes, her concern was evident, and my anger melted. And I knew why I was sitting in my office. It was because I knew I'd see her today. I knew that I *needed* to see her today, of all days. I didn't know why or understand it, but at the same time I did understand.

A HEALING TOUCH

Although, I was still confused about what had happened Friday night. I had wanted to text her or call her all weekend but something stopped me. She was frightened of something, and I didn't want her to run. She was super skittish right now, and I hoped that she'd relax.

I motioned her inside. She opened the door and sat in front of my desk. We sat there, staring at each other. The silence was so thick it was stifling.

"Is there something I can help you with?" I asked, my voice on edge. My head throbbed and I knew I was probably not going to last long. I needed to get some headache medicine in me quickly before it got further out of control. I didn't get headaches often but when I did, they were pretty strong, and it could turn into a migraine if I wasn't careful.

"Uh, well, first I want to say I'm sorry about Friday night."

"Sorry about what? You didn't do anything wrong."

"About freaking out on you when we were leaving."

"Oh, that." I smiled

"I'm not sure why I freaked out so bad. I didn't want you to think it was anything that you did because it wasn't. It was all me."

"Natasha, it's okay. Not a big deal. There's no need to get freaked out though when you are around me."

"I know that. I'm just umm....I'm just going through some stuff right now. I don't really want to talk about it. But, I wanted you to know that I am sorry that I lost my mind there for a few minutes. I don't want you to think that it would impact my work here in the office."

"It's done. Forgotten. Is there anything else I can help you with?"

"Kelsey told me a little bit about your sister. I'm so sorry. I didn't even know that you had a sister."

"Thanks. She was my little sister. I should have done a better job protecting her."

"You can't feel responsible for what happened."

"Well, I do. I knew something was wrong. But I ignored it. I was too busy. Too wrapped up in my projects and my friends. I didn't have time for her." I whispered.

Natasha sat there, and I wondered what was going through her mind. She shifted in her chair, moving closer to my desk, her hands settled on top of mine.

"I really am sorry, Troy. Nothing will be able to bring her back. I didn't know her. But I do know you, and I know that whatever happened it was not your fault."

With that, she stood and left my office. My hands still warm from her touch, I watched her walk to the break room. I was even more baffled. I couldn't wrap my head around this girl. One minute she was frightened out of her mind next to me. Then the next minute, she's placing her hands over mine and is concerned about how I'm feeling.

She was strong, and confident, and the next minute a deer in headlights. It didn't make any sense. And why was there something so familiar about her? I still couldn't put my fingers on it, and it was driving me insane.

The rest of the afternoon dragged. No one else even tried to approach me the rest of the afternoon. My phone was silent. Likely, the rest of the staff was fielding questions and not putting anyone through to my line. I tried to focus on the set of plans I was marking up, but it was useless. I don't know why I thought coming into the office was a good idea. But the other part of me didn't want to be by myself. I was tired of being alone.

Over the past few years, I had been so focused on school, work, and now all the licensing exams in front of me that I really hadn't had much of a social life. I'd dated, occasionally. A couple of the girls I'd dated had wanted more of a relationship, but I just wasn't there. I hadn't been ready for more than a casual relationship.

Lately though, my thoughts kept coming back to Natasha. There was something special about her. She was quiet and reserved, but passionate, and such a hard worker. She was focused and determined. Working in a male dominated field wasn't always easy. More and more women were getting into architecture and were very successful, but it was still predominantly men.

I'd looked forward to our staff dinners every Friday night. I hadn't missed one since Natasha had started coming. I knew I was walking a fine line though. Mixing social and work wasn't always the best. We could lose a really good employee if I pursued her and things went south. She could leave and go work with Caleb's family. The thought of that happening made me sick to my stomach. I knew that he had tried to get her to work for them. Now that I knew Natasha better, there's no way that I'd let that happen.

I picked up the red pen that was laying on the drawings and continued to add notes to the building section I was marking up. The construction documents for the Heely Residence were coming along really well.

Natasha had been a quick learner. Her attention to detail was amazing, and I appreciated only having to mark things up once. Not everyone that had worked with us over the years was like that. Many focused on how fast they could get drawings done. Instead, I'd spend wasted hours marking up the same notes again and again.

My headache had finally subsided after eating some lunch and taking some meds. There was still a lingering ache at my temples, but at least it was manageable. The ache was still strong enough to be annoying and distracting though. I might as well call it quits for the day. It had pretty much been a waste of my time even coming in. But in some ways, I felt like I'd finally started making some progress by even being here today.

Activity in the rest of the office indicated that everyone was wrapping up for the day. My gaze found its way, as it often did, to Natasha's desk. She was busy stacking up tile samples on the side of her desk. She really was stunning.

Her cheek bones angled down gracefully to her chin where she had a slight indention right in the center. She wore her hair down today with it sweeping to one side. She kept tucking strands behind her ears to keep it out of her face. Her head tilted up, and our eyes met. Without even thinking, I motioned her to my office.

"What's up?" she asked as the door shut behind her and she settled into one of the chairs across from my desk.

"Do you have plans for the rest of the evening?"

"Um. Not really. Why?"

"I need to go to the cemetery before it gets any later, and I really don't want to go by myself. I'll probably be super lousy company, but would you come with me?"

Several expressions fluttered across her face as she sat there. I wished that I could read her mind because right now I was beginning to wish I'd kept my big mouth shut.

If she was skittish before, this probably just pushed her over the edge. I wanted to kick myself. I needed to take baby steps with her, and this probably wasn't much of a baby step. More like a giant leap.

"Never mind. It's okay. I don't know what I was thinking. Why would you want to come out to the cemetery for someone you never knew?" The words just rushed out giving her a way out, so she didn't have to try to come up with a polite way to turn me down.

"Of course, I'll go Troy. I guess I was just a little surprised. I know it must be super personal and difficult for you. And I'd be happy to keep you company. I can't promise that I'll be much help though. I kind of suck at trying to cheer people up."

"Just being with me so I'm not alone is enough. I'm tired of being alone. Go ahead and finish up, and we'll head out. I'll bring you back here when we're done if that's okay?"

"Sure. I was almost done anyway. It will only be a few more minutes."

~ *Natasha* ~

Shutting down my computer, I tried to get my emotions under control. Troy's request had really surprised me. All summer working in the office, no one had ever mentioned anything about Troy's sister. Even conversations that I'd had with Troy had always been about work. I really didn't know much about his personal life except what Kelsey had mentioned. For him to ask me to keep him company on such a personal trip was actually a bit mind-boggling.

I knew how hard it had been for Bailey to move on after her entire family was killed. Mia and I had been there and watched her struggle to get through the pain and guilt of surviving. I'm sure what Troy was going through was somewhat similar. The loss of anyone that you loved was devastating. Especially someone with their entire life ahead of them.

Kelsey had already left. I saw Troy leaving his office. Pushing my chair up to my desk, I grabbed my purse and water bottle as Troy approached my desk.

"You ready?" he asked.

"Yes."

"After you," he said as he motioned to the front door.

Jordan was the last one in the office, and I could feel him watching us as we walked toward the front door. The weather was starting to cool down and a breeze had picked up. My sweater wasn't much barrier for the breeze, and I made a mental note that I needed to toss my jacket in my car.

"Are you cold?" Troy asked from beside me as we walked across the parking lot to his car.

"I'm okay. Thank you."

We reached his burgundy corvette and he clicked it open. It was an older model. I wasn't sure what year, but it was still beautiful. He walked to the passenger side and opened the door for me.

"There's no handles. It's all by touch. If you feel right here, it's like a touch pad. When you put your fingers flat on that area, it releases the door," Troy explained.

"Wow, that's crazy. What happens if the battery is dead? How do you get in?"

"There's a key hole in the back of the car. Then a lever in the trunk that will release the door."

I slid into the passenger seat, surprised by how much room I really had around my legs. Troy shut my door and it felt like it vacuumed shut. I'd never been inside a corvette before. It was a little overwhelming with all the buttons and gauges compared to my basic model car.

Troy settled into the driver's seat, pushed the start button and the car rumbled to life. The stereo was set on an eighties station, which somewhat surprised me.

"Eighties's huh?" I smiled.

"Of course. I listen to other stuff too, but that's my go-to." He smiled back.

Being so close to him, had all my senses on alert. I was scared and excited at the same time and wasn't sure how I could be feeling such opposite feelings. I snuck a quick glance in his direction as he pulled out of the office parking lot. The chill I had felt outside was gone.

His hair was a bit more tousled today. The stubble that covered his cheek bones was a lot darker than I'd ever seen it before. It didn't look like he'd shaved since Friday. The stubble though made his eyes stand out more. His dark, thick lashes framed his eyes. Today they looked gray.

When he looked at me, it was like he was seeing all the way through me, like I had no secrets. It was a bit unsettling.

Troy maneuvered the car through the downtown area, stopping at a florist shop just before they closed. I stayed in the car while he ran in. As I waited for him, my thoughts were running a mile a minute. When he returned, he had a small arrangement of daisies with him.

"Can you hold these for me?" he asked as he shut his door.

I reached over and took the wrapped flowers, my hands grazing his as he passed them over. The shock of his touch shot through my fingertips up my arm. I placed the flowers in my lap, careful to not bend the petals.

"Daisies were Talise's favorite flower. I take them every time I go to visit her grave. Did you know that daisies are actually made up of two separate flowers? The center is one flower and the petals around the outside are another flower." Troy explained as he backed the car out of the parking stall.

"I had no idea."

"I didn't either until the first time I bought them shortly after Talise passed. The florist mentioned it."

I looked down at the bouquet that sat in my lap. "They're very beautiful. So many different colors. When I think of daisies, I always think of white flowers with yellow centers. I never realized how many other colors there were."

"Talise always said they were cheerful flowers. She had planted a few in the backyard once when she was younger. But her gardening days didn't last long. She hated all the dirt under her fingernails. It used to drive her crazy."

The memory brought a slight smile to his face as he glanced over catching me as I watched him. I felt my face flash on fire as I quickly turned back to look out the windshield.

A HEALING TOUCH

Our drive was short and was silent the rest of the way. The smell of the daisies filled the small interior of the car. Troy drove with ease, but I could tell he was tense. His entire body was rigid, and every once in a while, I caught a slight twitch in his jaw. When I glanced over at him, I didn't even know what to say.

When we reached the cemetery, Troy drove through the winding road until he reached what appeared to be the back part of the cemetery. He pulled along the side of the road and turned off the car.

I reached for the door handle to let myself out when I felt his hand rest on top of my hand that held the wrapped daisies. Turning to look at him, I found myself lost in his eyes. I'd never seen him so emotional before.

"Thank you again for coming with me."

"You're welcome."

His hand was warm on mine. It lingered slightly before he pulled it away. He grabbed his key fob and then opened his door. I pushed the passenger door open, extracting myself from the low seat of the corvette with the wrapped daisies held tightly in my hand. Troy waited for me at the front of the car. When I reached him, he started walking across the green grass scattered with stone markers.

The wind had picked up, and the breeze whipped my hair against my face. My sweater was no match against the cool evening, and I tried to hold back the shiver that traveled through my body. We passed through a small seating area surrounded by trees and continued a few more feet when he stopped. He reached for the bouquet, and I handed them over.

The stone marker was covered with fresh flowers, but I could glimpse a colored photo that was embedded

Melissa A. Hanson

in the stone. Troy's hair was dark brown. Even Camille's was dark, and while Thomas's was mostly gray, he had dark, almost black roots. Talise had dark red hair. Her facial features were much like Camille's, but her eyes were so much like Troy's it was unsettling.

She had been beautiful, and I wondered what had been so bad in her life that she didn't want to live any more. Even the pain I'd been through recently and the dark days I'd found myself in I'd never gotten to the point where I had wanted to end my life. I knew that in comparison to what I was going through there were others in the world that had it so much worse than I did.

Ultimately, I wasn't going to let someone else's decisions destroy me. I wouldn't give them that power over me, but it was still hard to get through some days. The darkness clawing to get in and consume me was something I still fought against.

Troy placed the daisies with the rest of the flowers, and then stepped back so that he was standing next to me. I looked up at him and my heart broke. His eyes had filled with tears and one had slipped down his cheek. I reached over and gently wiped it away.

"I'm so sorry, Troy." I didn't know what else to say. My hand slipped from his cheek to settle on his arm. I watched as more tears trickled down his cheeks as his eyes never left mine.

"I should have done more. She should still be here. It was my fault. She had tried to reach out to me a couple of times those weeks before she passed and I was too busy and always just pushed it aside. And she never pushed, she just let it go and would smile and say 'okay, it's not a big deal, it can wait'.

"I had no idea Natasha, no idea how bad she had been feeling. I don't even know what turned everything

136

so bad. She never said anything to her friends. Nothing. She didn't leave a note. Nothing."

"It's not your fault Troy, and you can't beat yourself up about it. You can't change the past; you can only move forward. You learn from the past, you grow, and you become stronger. Each of us has a choice. She made a choice and it's not your fault."

I felt Troy shift and his arms came around me, lightly pulling me ever so gently against his chest. My arms slid up his back as he hugged me tight.

"How did you get so wise?" he whispered into my hair, his breath warm on my neck as he leaned closer.

"I'm not. I struggle every day. But I watched my friend Bailey recover from the loss of her family. And I watched my friend Mia, survive a thirty-two-foot fall from a chairlift and fight for her life. Both of them were able to fight their demons and move on. If they can do it, anyone can."

He pulled back and looked at me. "Thirty-two feet? Your friend fell thirty-two feet from a chairlift?"

"Yeah, last Thanksgiving actually. It was touch and go for a while, but she survived."

"Wow, that's incredible."

"It really was, it was one of my most frightening moments not knowing if she was going to pull through."

Another gust of wind picked up and this time I wasn't able to hide my shiver.

"Let's go. You don't need to get sick on me."

We walked back across the grass, full of other's loved ones laid to rest. Some stones surrounded by flowers and trinkets, and others that looked to be over grown and ancient. The sun was beginning to set and the sky was painted pinks and deep oranges. A few white clouds spotted across the horizon.

When we reached the corvette, Troy unlocked the car and I anxiously climbed in to get out of the wind. Troy started the car and made sure the heater was on the highest setting.

"It should warm up pretty quick," he said as he put the car in gear and maneuvered out of the cemetery back towards town.

We were driving through a part of town I hadn't explored much. Even though I'd been in Eugene for a year now, school kept me so busy I didn't get out much beyond the radius of the school and downtown area. The greenery was so different here in Oregon, it was so beautiful with lots of trees and one of the biggest reasons why I'd chosen to attend school here.

"Are you hungry?" Troy asked.

"A little bit."

"Would you like to stop and get something to eat with me?"

I smiled. "Sure, that would be great." I knew it was just dinner and probably meant nothing. But I really enjoyed Troy's company, and a chance to spend a little longer with him before I had to go back to my dorm. I'd take it in a heartbeat.

~ *Troy* ~

Natasha's presence had made my cemetery visit so much easier. Today she seemed much stronger, and more confident. Not the timid and shy girl that had been around the office most of the summer. Every instinct in my body was telling me that this was the real Natasha. That the skittish one I'd witnessed several times over the summer wasn't. Something had happened to her in the recent past that had caused her to be frightened of something. I hoped that she would continue to feel safe with me.

Hugging her in at the cemetery had been instinctive. For a second, I was worried that she was going to freak out with the contact like she had Friday night when I touched her cheek; but she didn't. She had hugged me back and it had felt right. Like she belonged there in my arms. It was the first time I'd ever felt that strong of a connection with a girl. All the others before her, had never felt the same.

"Is Mexican okay?" I asked, while I glanced at her.

She smiled, "I love Mexican."

"Awesome, I know the perfect place."

The food was amazing as it always was. Natasha had talked all the way through dinner. I had learned about her older brother Quinn who was still back in her hometown of Riverview.

I'd also learned more about her best friends Bailey and Mia. Mia and Natasha had grown up together. Bailey had moved to Riverview their junior year of high school to live with her aunt and uncle after her family had been killed. Bailey was now in Las Vegas going to college to be near her boyfriend Collin.

Mia was still in Riverview and was dating Dylan who was part of the local mountain ski patrol. They had met when she had almost died the previous Thanksgiving after falling from a chair lift while skiing. Dylan was one of the first patrol on the scene and had kept coming to see her at the hospital while she recovered.

I sat and listened, amazed by her friends. They seemed to be very close. The ski lift accident was mind boggling. Even hearing Natasha tell the story it was unbelievable. It was like a tale straight from fiction. Mia really, had been incredibly lucky.

Natasha talked about the adjustment from living in Southern California to Oregon. She had been super homesick when she first started school and missed her friends. How she had gotten along immediately with her roommate Justine and that friendship had helped ease the homesickness.

I knew from her portfolio that she wasn't going to have any problems in school. She had picked up and learned so much even during the summer that she was going to do well. While Architecture school was intense, I knew she was going to be able to handle it and work. She had that determination in her, that strive for more. She settled for nothing but the best.

Natasha had asked several questions about Kelsey and why we'd never dated. I told her how Kelsey and I had gone through school together. We'd always clicked well but it was more on a sibling level. We hung out a lot and worked well together, but it was never more than that. I could sense relief in Natasha, and it made me smile.

She obviously had been concerned if there was anything going on between Kelsey and myself. She had carefully then asked if there was someone else in the picture that I was seeing, and I could almost see her holding her breath while she waited for the answer. Her breath releasing when I confirmed that there wasn't anyone I'd been dating, made me smile.

After dinner was finished we sat and talked. Talking with her was easy. I felt I could tell her anything. It wasn't forced and I didn't want the evening to end. When she yawned, I knew it was probably time to go.

Walking back to my car, my hand rested lightly on her lower back. She didn't pull away, and I figured that was a good sign, but I knew I needed to take it slow with her. I needed to unravel why she had been so freaked out before. I didn't want to repeat the same mistake.

The drive back to the office was quick. I pulled into the parking lot and parked next to her car. She reached for her purse and pulled her keys out. My hand covered hers as it laid in her lap.

"Thank you again for coming with me."

"I'm not sure I was much company. But I enjoyed spending time with you, and thank you for dinner."

"I enjoyed the time with you as well. Would you want to do it again?" I asked, hoping I wasn't pushing things too fast.

"Sure, I'd really like that." She smiled and then pushed open the passenger door.

She unlocked her car and then leaned down before shutting the passenger door. "I'll see you tomorrow."

"Goodnight Natasha."

"'Night Troy."

CHAPTER FOURTEEN

~ Natasha ~

School had started and I'd hit the ground running. I'd now officially completed my first week as a second-year architecture student. My classes were packed and it was going to be an intense year. This year not only did I have my classes I needed to worry about, but I was squeezing in work as well.

I was excited though to have the opportunity to stay at DeLuca Architects, and I wasn't going to lie to myself. Seeing Troy throughout the week was a huge bonus.

After the evening at the cemetery, Troy and I had talked and texted pretty much every night. I enjoyed our time together, and every day I craved it more. I felt like I was starting to get myself back, and the dark cloud that had swirled around me most of the summer was beginning to lift.

I wasn't sure at what point exactly the shift started taking place, and to be honest I really didn't care. I was tired of being scared and worrying about something I couldn't change. I knew I needed to move forward and let it go.

I had yet to run into Caleb, and part of me was relieved. How weird that within a few months' things had changed so much. Before, I'd looked forward to seeing him and getting his help, but after the last couple of times I'd seen him I was okay not running into him.

With my school schedule, I was working Tuesday's and Thursday's and spent most of Monday, Wednesday, and Friday's in class and homework. Wednesday's were the hardest day with classes stacked from noon until six thirty at night.

Class was finally over, and I was gathering my things. Troy was picking me up from the dorm in thirty minutes so we could go to our weekly Friday dinner with the office. I wanted to have a few minutes to touch up my makeup and change before he arrived. I closed my laptop, and was sliding it into my bag, when a folded note slipped out from under it.

I unfolded it, and as I started reading the short note, I felt like the whole room shifted and I was quickly spiraling back under the dark cloud that I'd been fighting so hard to get rid of.

Your new boyfriend will never be able to claim what I've already claimed.

Looking around the room, no one appeared to be watching me. But I felt like I was being watched. Spied on. I finished grabbing the rest of my things and practically ran out of the building. It was getting harder to breath and I needed to get back to my room. Tears threatened to escape and I was fighting to keep them at bay.

All I could focus on was getting to safety. I needed to get away from here. The short walk to the dorm was a blur. I kept telling myself just one foot in front of the other. My room wasn't much further. I was laser focused on reaching the dorm when strong arms wrapped around me, I screamed. My panic was in full force now and I was in flight mode.

"Natasha, calm down. It's just me. What happened? Are you okay?"

Troy's voice was worried, and it snapped me out of my panic for at least a minute to be able to grab a breath.

"I can't, I can't," I cried. I knew I wasn't making any sense and the tears were streaming down my face.

"Natasha, please, calm down. It's okay. I'm not going to let anyone hurt you. Do you want to go back to your room or do you want to go to my car?"

"My room, please." I looked up into Troy's face and I could see he was worried and confused.

His arms pulled me tight against him as he walked me the rest of the way to my room in silence. I unlocked my door and was relieved to find it empty. I laid my backpack and laptop bag on my desk. Troy shut and locked the door behind him. I felt his arms gently turn me and pull me against his chest into a tight hug.

"Please tell me what's wrong. What happened?" He asked.

I couldn't hold it in anymore. I felt myself shatter and fall apart in his arms. I started to cry, hysterical tears, sobbing, soaking the front of his shirt with I'm sure was both snot and tears. But I couldn't stop. Troy held me tight, stroking my hair.

"Shhh. It's going to be okay," he whispered.

"No, no it's never going to be okay," I cried, hiccuping as I uttered the words.

"It is. Just like you told me the other day, things always get better."

A HEALING TOUCH

I held onto him like my life depended on it. When did I become so attached to him? When did I start to feel so safe when I was with him? I didn't know.

All I knew was that right now in this moment I did feel safe and protected, but I was scared and rattled at what was outside my dorm room. What monster still hunted me? Why wouldn't he leave me alone?

"Come, sit. Which bed is yours?" he asked.

I pointed to my bed that was against the outside wall, under the window and he gently guided me to it. He sat against the pillows with his legs open and pulled me carefully in front of him, my back propped against his chest. I felt his arms wrap around me and pull me tight. His chin settled on top of my head. My arms wrapped over the top of his, my fingers interlaced with his. My tears continued to stream down my face. I leaned my head sideways so that it rested against his heart.

"Natasha, please baby, tell me what's wrong."

"You don't want to know. You won't want anything to do with me."

"That's not true. There's nothing that you could say that would push me away like that."

"You say that now, but you don't know. You don't know," I cried.

"I promise. Please. I'm not going anywhere. Let me help you."

"Please, just hold me," I begged.

"I am. I'm here."

I felt his arms tighten around me as he gently kissed the top of my head while I cried and cried until I didn't think I had any more tears left to shed. His arms gave me shelter and protection. I never wanted to leave them.

I'm not sure how long we sat there as the sun sank in the distance and the room darkened. My eyes burned and felt swollen. I'm sure they were puffy and I knew I probably looked even worse than I felt.

"I'm sorry. I've soaked your shirt." I sat up and shifted so that I could face him. I leaned over and flipped on the light attached to the side of my bed to give us a little light in the room. I didn't want to get off the bed to turn the main light on.

"I don't care." His fingertips reached for my face and gently wiped away the wetness that still lingered.

"Natasha, something is really wrong. Please talk to me. I promise, I'm not going to run. I don't know about you, but these last few weeks you've really become someone important in my life. I don't want to lose you. Not when we've just started to get to know each other better."

I sat there my eyes searching his. Wondering what to even say. I wasn't sure if I could utter the words to him. He said it didn't matter but what if it did when he found out. But maybe it was better to find that out now, before I got even more attached to him and the pain of him walking away later would be so much worse. I was so confused and conflicted.

"I don't even know where to start." I sighed.

"At the beginning. I promise. Nothing you say to me is going to make me run."

"We'll see." I pushed back slightly which allowed me to face him. My knees were bent in front of me and my arms wrapped around them holding on for dear life.

I sat there silently watching him, backed up against the other end of the bed. Running every scenario through my head, I was torn, not knowing what to do. I took a deep breath and let it out.

A HEALING TOUCH

"It was at the end of spring quarter. I went to a party with Justine. I didn't really want to, but she'd begged me to come with her. I drove. The party sucked, and I was ready to go home. Everyone was drinking, but I only grabbed a bottle of water. The next thing I remembered was that the room was spinning. After that, my next memory was waking up the following morning upstairs in one of the bedrooms. My underwear was on the floor. I have no memory of what happened. I grabbed my stuff that was next to me and ran.

"I got back to the dorm and Justine was in a panic. She'd been trying to reach me all night. When I went to the bathroom, there was evidence that I'd been raped. Justine took me to the hospital and they collected what evidence they could. But since I have no memory of anything there's really nothing they can do."

I watched Troy's face for signs of revulsion, or getting ready to run, but all I saw was sadness and concern.

"Troy, I'd never been with anyone before. I know that's crazy these days. A freshman in college and still a virgin. But I was. I'd never been with anyone before. Whoever raped me that night took my virginity. I'll never get that back. I'll never be able to offer that to someone I love. I had no say."

The tears had pooled and once again dripped from the sides of my eyes, streaming down my face. I tried to wipe them away, but more just took their place.

"Come here." His arms were outstretched, and I climbed into his open arms and held on. Quiet sobs still shook me.

"Natasha, it wasn't your fault. I'm so sorry you had to go through that. Why did you think I'd run?"

"Because, I feel dirty. I'm tainted now and I don't even know who it was. He's out there Troy. And he's watching me and it scares me to death. It could be anyone and I'll never know. I'll never know who it was."

"What freaked you out so bad tonight? What happened?"

"Monday, after the party, I was back in class and there was a note left for me at my work area. It basically said he knew he'd taken my virginity. It freaked me out that he knew where my class was. It meant it was someone who knew me. Not some stranger I didn't know at the party. All summer there's been nothing. I thought, I guess stupidly, that maybe he'd decided to leave me alone, or maybe he wasn't around anymore. Maybe he'd graduated or moved away. But then tonight when I was putting away my stuff after class there was another note. He knows I've been seeing you. How? How would anyone know that unless he's been spying on me."

"What did the note say? Was it typed or handwritten?" Troy asked.

"It was hand printed. It said *Your new boyfriend will never be able to claim what I've already claimed.*'"

"Was there a police report filed?"

"Yes," I answered.

"Then you need to take the note to them because now it's more than one event that happened. This is stalking Natasha and it's not okay."

"I just wanted the whole thing to go away."

"I know, but you can't let someone frighten you like that." He pulled back so that he could look at me. "I'll go with you. You don't have to do this alone."

"I don't want to take anything to the police right now. I mean it's just notes. What are they going to do?

They're just going to ask me a bunch of questions that I can't answer right now."

"I really think you should let them know. But I'm not going to push you. I'm here for you. Anytime you decide to go, I will go with you. Okay?"

I nodded. "Thank you."

"I don't think I feel like going out anymore. How 'bout we just grab something to go?"

"Pizza? Pizza is always a good choice." I smiled. I knew I must look awful. My eyes were probably puffy and red but Troy was still sitting here by my side. That had to be a good sign, right? And at that moment, I felt like the last of the weight I'd been carrying around with me was lifted and that felt good too. It felt very, very good.

We were sitting on my bed cross-legged with the pizza box between us when Justine came in. She looked shocked, her eyes darting to Troy and back to me.

"Uh, I can come back if you want me to?" Justine asked.

"You can join us if you'd like, there's plenty." I offered.

"Nice to see you again Justine." Troy stated as Justine walked over to grab a piece of pizza. She stopped just in front of me staring.

"Holy crap Natasha, you look horrible. What happened? Are you okay?"

I knew Justine wouldn't let my puffy eyes go without saying something.

"I got another note at the end of class today. Similar to the other one." I answered her.

Justine's eyes darted from mine to Troy's. I knew she was trying to figure out how to respond or what to say.

"Troy knows. I told him." I answered her silent question.

"Everything?" she asked.

"Yeah, I told him everything."

"Okay then. What are you going to do about the note?" Justine asked as she grabbed her slice of pizza and started chewing. She grabbed a chair from our desk area and slid it near my bed where we were sitting.

"Nothing," I answered.

"Seriously?" she responded.

"For now, yes. Think about it Justine, what do I have? Two notes. I have no idea who sent them. What are they going to do about it? For now, I'm going to leave it be. Whoever is sending them is probably just trying to get me upset and he's doing a good job. But if I can ignore it, isn't that better? For now, I'll just be more aware of who I'm around and make sure I'm not alone."

"You're taking this a whole lot better than I would have thought." Justine stated.

"You should have seen me an hour ago. It wasn't pretty. Ask Troy he got the brunt of it."

"I'm just giving you fair warning Troy. Natasha has been through enough these last few months. If you hurt my friend in any way, you're going to have to deal with me."

Troy chuckled. "I hear you loud and clear. But trust me I'm not here to hurt her."

A HEALING TOUCH

~ *Troy* ~

After finishing the pizza and talking a bit with Justine, she left to study in the library with her study group. I laid back against Natasha's pillows as she laid between my legs, her head resting on my chest. We were watching a movie on her iPad which she had propped up on the window sill above her bed.

Near the end of the movie her head nodded to the side and I realized she had fallen asleep. My arms were wrapped around her and I held her while she rested. After all the crying she had done tonight, I figured she was probably exhausted.

I had my suspicions for a while now that something bad had happened to her. Hearing her say the words out loud though shattered my heart. How could anyone do something like that to her?

I was glad I'd arrived at her dorm early tonight. I'd finished up what I had been working on a little early and I'd just planned to wait for her at the front lobby of her dorm. When I saw her practically running to the dorm, I knew something was wrong.

When she landed in my arms, she was nearly hysterical and my heart broke. I had instinctively looked around to see if someone had been chasing her. All I wanted to do at that moment was to protect her and get her to safety and calmed down.

Kissing the top of her head, I tried not to move. I'd let her sleep for a bit before I left. I wasn't ready to leave her yet. Her breathing had evened out, several strands of her hair had drifted across her face and I carefully tucked them behind her ear.

So many things now were falling into place. Why some minutes she was scared out of her mind, while others she was strong and confident. I knew she needed someone to be there for her and I was determined to be that person for her. Now more than ever, I just hoped that she would let me and not push me away. At least I had a better sense of what I was dealing with now, and knew I'd have to take things slowly and carefully with her.

I woke up to Natasha crying out in her sleep. I had no idea what time it was or how long I'd even been asleep. Gently, I rubbed her arms trying to wake her.

"Natasha, baby, wake up. You're dreaming."

"No. No. Stay away from me." Natasha's voice was getting louder as she thrashed in my arms pushing away from me.

"Whoa, it's just me, Troy. Natasha, wake up."

She pushed away from me, sitting up, tears trickling down her cheeks. Finally, recognition lit her eyes and I knew she was fully awake.

"You fell asleep. You were having a bad dream. It was just a dream, Natasha."

Sobs started to wrack her body again as she leaned forward and clung to me. Her arms wrapped around my back. Her head rested against my chest.

"I'm sorry, Troy. It was so real. But I can't even tell you what I was dreaming. Only that I was scared. So, so, scared."

"Shh. It's okay. I'm right here."

"Please don't leave me tonight. Can you just stay here with me and hold me? Please."

"I'm not leaving you. Let me slide down into a more comfortable spot though. If I lay like this all night, I'm going to wake up with a horrible kink in my neck." I slid down so I was laying on my side with my back against the wall and pulled her against me. I draped my arm around her middle, holding tight. "Try to go back to sleep, okay?"

I felt her nod, her sobs finally subsiding. This wasn't how I had planned to spend this evening. While I hated that she was going through so much pain, being able to hold her like this was nothing to complain about.

Settling my head against hers, she started to relax, and her fingers intertwined with mine as we lay there and drifted to sleep.

~ *Natasha* ~

Sun was streaming into my room. I was warm, wrapped tightly in my blanket, rolling over I ran into the hard chest of Troy and realized it wasn't the warmth from my blanket that I was feeling, but the warmth of Troy's body against mine. His arm was wrapped around me. I felt at home, secure.

I'd never fallen asleep beside any guy before, this was a first for me. I lay there facing him while he slept, studying his handsome features. I couldn't believe how lucky I was that our paths had crossed. And that even after everything I'd told him last night he was still here by my side.

He rolled to his back, and I snuggled against his side, my head resting on his chest. My arm draped across his torso. Closing my eyes, I drifted quickly back to sleep.

Natasha picked up the note and the horror that came across her face was priceless. She thought she could escape from me? It wasn't going to be that easy.

I was still here.

Watching. Waiting.

Waiting for the perfect moment for her to be mine again. No one was going to stand in my way. It didn't have to be this way. But she wanted to play hard to get now, so game on.

CHAPTER FIFTEEN

~ *Natasha* ~

Staring at my reflection in the mirror, I realized that I no longer had deep shadows under my eyes. The face that stared back at me was one I recognized. Not the shell of who I'd been all summer long. I had taken care with my makeup today. My long, dark hair hung in loose curls around my shoulders.

Justine and I had gone shopping and I'd found a gorgeous wine-colored dress. It was sophisticated, classy, with a touch of sexy. It was form fitting, short cap sleeves, and a V neck with the fabric wrapping to the side with an asymmetrical hem.

I wore a simple white gold necklace and dangle earrings. Tonight, I was attending an architectural awards dinner with Troy and the rest of the office. It was a regional annual awards dinner where projects from around the area were acknowledged. DeLuca Architects had two projects this year that had been nominated.

The last six weeks had been a crazy whirlwind of activity. Balancing work, school and spending time with Troy had me going every minute of every day. But I loved it, I was feeling more confident in myself again, more carefree and putting the past in the past.

Troy had been so supportive and understanding of some of my crazy mood swings that still struck me. Sometimes I never even knew what would set off an emotional breakdown. A smell, a sight, something in my subconscious would trigger a defensive response and there was no rationale. Troy took it all in stride. Even if we were in public, he'd carefully get me out of wherever we were until I could calm down.

I knew I was falling hard for him. Every day, every minute we spent time together that bond grew deeper. His text messages always made me smile. Little notes he'd leave for me on my desk at work always brightened my day. I couldn't believe how lucky I'd gotten.

"Wow, Natasha, you look amazing!" Justine's voice from behind snapped me out of my thoughts.

I caught her gaze in the mirror as I turned around to face her.

"Thanks, I haven't been this dressed up since…I can't even remember." I laughed.

"Well, you're sure going to turn heads tonight. That dress fits you perfect."

"Thanks. I'm glad you found it buried on the racks. I was beginning to think I wouldn't be able to find anything that I liked."

"Troy isn't going to be able to stop staring at you. You really look amazing Natasha."

"Thanks, I hope he does like it. He should be here shortly to pick me up. I better finish grabbing my things."

Leaving the bathroom, I began pulling the few items that I'd need out of my regular purse into a small silver clutch. I had a lightweight silver sweater to help with the cooler temps that October had brought. Hopefully, it would be enough to ward off the chill.

A HEALING TOUCH

Knocking on our door brought a smile to my face and I was anxious to see what Troy thought. Justine had moved to her bed and was propped up against her pillows with her laptop. As I opened the door, Troy's handsome face smiled at me, warming me down to my toes. It was crazy how one look could affect me so much.

"Natasha, you look stunning."

"Thanks, you look pretty handsome yourself."

Troy was dressed in slacks, dress shirt and jacket, but slightly casual by not wearing a tie. His shirt unbuttoned at the top gave him a reckless but stunning look. Dressed up, but sporting a bit of a rebel side. I stepped aside so that Troy could enter the room while I grabbed my things.

"Hi Justine. How's it going?" Troy asked.

"It's going. Cramming for a test on Monday. It's going to be a sucky weekend," Justine replied.

"Sorry about that. I'm sure you'll do just fine. Natasha, are you ready?" Troy asked.

"I am. See you later Justine," I said as I followed Troy out the door.

"See you both later. Have fun!" Justine called from her bed.

Locking the door behind me, I tossed my keys in my clutch, and smiled up at Troy. "What?" I asked him.

"You look amazing. I'm not going to be able to take my eyes off of you all night. Well, I mean you always look amazing, but tonight there's something different about you. Not just being dressed up, but something else."

"I feel good. I feel like I'm finally getting myself back and I can't tell you how relieved that makes me. I was really scared that I'd never feel like myself again."

Troy turned me slightly so I was directly facing him. I was closer to eye level tonight with my silver heels. His gaze pierced through to my soul. I felt his hands slide against the side of my neck holding my head gently as he leaned down and kissed me. His warm lips on mine, I could taste the mint from his toothpaste. My hands slid around his waist as I snuggled into his embrace. He deepened the kiss and I welcomed the intrusion. I could stand here forever in his arms. He pulled back slightly, his forehead resting against mine.

"Come on, we better get going," Troy said as he pulled away. His hand reached out for mine and we walked hand in hand to his car.

The drive to the event center took a little under thirty minutes as we winded our way from city streets into the country landscape reaching the edge of a nearby lake. The music played in the background as we discussed the event and the awards that DeLuca Architects were up for.

Troy's hand rested on the gear shift; his fingers interlaced with mine. I glanced over at his strong profile. It was confident and handsome. He sensed me staring at him and his eyes caught mine, his lips curling into a smile.

"What?" He asked, his head turning back to focus on the road ahead of us.

"Nothing. I was just looking." I smiled.

He laughed, his hand tightening around mine, he quickly brought it to his lips and brushed a light kiss on the top of my hand. Goosebumps raced up my arms, causing me to shiver.

"Are you cold? I can turn the heat up."

"No, I'm okay. That's just the affect that you have on me."

"I make you cold?" he teased.

"No." I laughed. "You know exactly what I'm talking about."

"I know. I just wanted to hear you say it." He smiled.

"You're awful, you know that." I teased back.

"I know, and I'm afraid you're stuck with me. You probably should have run for the hills while you had the chance," he joked.

"What am I going to do with you?"

"Hmm…. That might be a dangerous question."

"Troy!"

He laughed and I loved how he laughed. It always brightened my day.

Trees lined the sides of the two-lane road and we turned into a small parking area that was already over halfway filled up. A large wood framed structure sat on the edge of the lot. It was a quaint building with giant wood timber trusses.

Generous grass areas intermingled with planter areas, the forest not far away in the background. The area was lit with vintage looking light standards that followed several paths as they meandered through the area connecting small seating areas. There were several beautiful photo opportunities. It was a perfect venue for weddings and events.

Troy's arm rested gently against my back as we walked to the building. We entered a large open meeting space. It was filled with round tables; navy table clothes and silver accents completed the layout. A small stage was located at one end of the room with a large screen that displayed several of the building projects that were nominated for the awards.

The room had a large, vaulted ceiling with the same heavy timber open trusses that were visible from the exterior supporting the roof. Large ceiling fans with lights were positioned between the trusses. Small square wood framed windows were located around the building providing glimpses into the surrounding landscaping.

Camille and Thomas were standing across the room and motioned for us to join them. Camille gave me a quick hug and then gave Troy a quick peck on the cheek. It warmed my heart to see the obvious affection that his family was willing to express in public.

Camille was dressed in an elegant, simple navy, sheath dress with a side slit. Thomas sported a full three-piece suit. I was so used to seeing him more casual in the office but the full suit fit him well.

Troy pulled my chair out for me as we reached our chairs. Alex and his fiancé, Alyssa were already seated at the table with Evan and his wife, Jennifer

"Hi guys," I greeted them as I sat.

"Hey Natasha. Welcome to your first award event," Evan said.

"Thanks. This is a really cool building. Do they do the event here every year?" I asked.

"They've done them here the last couple of years, but before that it was a different place each year. This one has been the favorite though by far."

"It's gorgeous. The grounds are amazing outside too."

"There's an open covered patio area in the back too. Alex and I have been to a wedding here and they had it all decorated with twinkling lights and it was so pretty. We're thinking about having our wedding here, if I can get Alex to ever commit to a day," Alyssa teased as she leaned against her fiancé.

The room was filling up quickly, waiters brought drinks and bread to the table. Kelsey, Jordan, and his wife Lisa were still missing. Kelsey was always running late, so her missing was nothing new. Conversation at the table was light and teasing. I loved how everyone got along. It really was more than just an office, it was a family.

Troy's hand rested on my knee and it made me feel grounded and safe. The chair next to me slid from the table and Kelsey plopped down with a heavy sigh.

"About time you finally made an appearance," I joked with her.

"Yeah, well, let's just say I was not having a good day," Kelsey said as she settled in next to me.

"Sorry, you look fantastic, though."

Kelsey always looked great. I don't think I'd ever seen her not looking stunning. Her confidence and personality also made her stand out in a crowd. I was still surprised some special guy hadn't won her heart yet.

"Thanks. You're looking pretty fabulous yourself. Where's Jordan and Lisa?" Kelsey asked as she looked around the table.

"Not sure, they haven't shown up yet," I answered.

"Actually, Jordan and Lisa aren't going to be able to make it," Camille said from across the table.

"What happened to them?" Kelsey asked.

"Kids are sick. Lisa called a little bit ago. They were all dressed and ready to walk out the door when their youngest started throwing up. She had told Jordan to go without her but before he left their oldest wasn't feeling so well either. Jordan decided it was better to stay with Lisa, and he wasn't sure if he'd end up exposing us to whatever the kids had," Camille explained.

Dinner was finished, and the awards program was about ready to get started. I was stuffed. The food had been amazing, which I hadn't been expecting. All the water and diet coke I'd been drinking had gone straight through me. I needed to get to the bathroom before the program got underway.

Kelsey and Evan were in a lively discussion about some difference in opinions about the design of a kitchen and it made me smile. I was pretty sure Evan was going to lose that battle.

"I'll be right back. I need to use the ladies' room," I whispered to Troy as I pushed back my chair and grabbed my clutch.

"Okay. It's just down the hallway off the entry, the women's restroom is at the end."

"Thanks."

I walked carefully around the round tables. I was surprised at how many people had come, but I realized it wasn't just architecture firms. There were all the engineering firms, civil, landscape, mechanical, plumbing, electrical, and structural too that had worked on the nominated projects. They had been just as important in the design as the architecture firm. There were a few familiar faces I had seen in our office or on the couple of construction sites that I'd been able to visit during the summer.

A HEALING TOUCH

The hallway to the bathroom winded around the corner. A few small groups of people stood talking in the lobby area. I followed the hallway down to the end. Thankfully, the women's restroom wasn't full.

It never failed now when I was in large restrooms, I always looked around at all the details. How different code issues were addressed, where they obvious, or was it a unique way to address the typical design problems we had to solve with bathroom designs. I found myself often taking photos of different solutions as a reference for future projects. Justine always thought I was crazy when she'd catch me taking photos and was constantly teasing me about it.

The lighting in this bathroom was bright and the back lighting around the mirrors over the counter was something I hadn't seen before. It looked like the mirror was set away from the wall and then light around the edge illuminated through a sandblasted portion that framed the mirror. It was a cool little detail and I snapped a few pictures.

After washing my hands, I wiped the lingering water spots from the counter. Puddles of water sitting on counters was one of my pet peeves, it totally drove me nuts. I touched up my lipstick and then left the restroom.

My heals clicked on the wood plank flooring as I walked, a slight echo throughout the wood framed structure. Just before I reached the lobby, there was another hallway that led to the rear of the building. It opened up to a large vaulted patio, which must be the space that Alyssa had been talking about. She hadn't been joking. It was beautiful and even more so if it was completely decorated.

I was so focused on the view to the outside, the grasp on my arm startled me. I jumped back, stumbling and bumping into a small table that held a glass vase with a beautiful floral arrangement. Thankfully, the vase wobbled but stayed upright.

"Caleb. What are you doing here?" I asked. I hadn't seen him at all since school started which was unusual. Especially since I'd seen him pretty much every day last year.

"Same thing you are. DeLuca Architects isn't the only firm that got nominated for awards. You should have come to work for us. You would have had so many more opportunities." His words were slow and slightly slurred.

The smell of alcohol on him was strong. His normally clear brown eyes were bloodshot. I was beginning to feel uncomfortable and trapped. I quickly looked down the hall, but we were just out of sight of the lobby and the hallway had emptied. They were probably getting ready to start the program. We seemed to be alone in the hall.

"I should get back to the table. It was good seeing you Caleb." I held my clutch tightly in my grasp and tried to walk past him.

His arm reached out and stopped me in my tracks. "You're so beautiful, Natasha. Why are you with Troy? He doesn't deserve you, I'm the one that helped you all year last year."

The grip on my arm tightened and my heart was racing. I needed to get out of here and fast. "I thought we were just friends. You never asked me out." I was frantic to calm him. I could sense his agitation and the alcohol, I knew wasn't helping the situation. This wasn't the fun, carefree guy I had seen last year, and that I'd been crushing on.

While one hand still held me in place, his other hand reached up, and he ran his fingers down the side of my face. My skin crawled with his touch. "Caleb, please let me go. You're hurting me," I begged as I tried to pull away from him. I could feel my control slipping quickly away. It was getting harder and harder to breathe.

"Troy's no good for you. You'll see. All he cares about is his work. No one else, not even his own sister. Did you even know he had a sister? She's dead now though. Gone. She was so beautiful. She's dead because of him."

I could feel the room start to spin. I tried to focus, to stay calm. But it wasn't working and I was losing control faster than I could reign it in. Caleb wasn't making any sense, and I was starting to lose my control. The darkness was chasing me and it was going to win if I couldn't escape it.

"It wasn't Troy's fault. She ended her own life."

"That's what he wants you to think. But he could have saved her. He didn't because he was too selfish, too wrapped up in himself. He'll never be there for you, just like he was never there for his sister."

"Caleb, please, just let me go."

Caleb towered over me. He had to be even a few inches taller than Troy. He leaned in closer to my face, my body pushed up against the wall behind me as I tried to back away from him. I was starting to shake uncontrollably. My breathing was getting harder to slow down and I felt like everything was spinning. Everything around me was starting to get blurry.

Caleb was saying something, but I couldn't understand what he was saying. My arm was beginning to burn where he held onto it. I was having trouble getting air into my lungs, my panic intensified and I didn't know how to escape.

~ *Troy* ~

Natasha should have been back by now. I was beginning to get worried. I kept looking towards the back of the room waiting for her to appear. The presentation had started and everyone was focused on the projection screen and the speaker at the front of the room. But something wasn't right. I could feel it.

I leaned over to Kelsey. "I'll be right back. I'm going to make sure Natasha is okay."

As I stood up my mom gave me a questioning look, but turned back toward the front of the room. I quickly maneuvered around the tables and into the empty lobby.

Looking around, there was no sign of Natasha. I turned down the hallway that led to the bathrooms, about halfway down I heard voices. I reached the hallway that led to the rear of the building and my heart stopped.

All I could see was red. Natasha was pushed up against the wall with Caleb's hands grasping her arm and his other hand on the side of her face.

Anger flooded my body and all I wanted to do at that moment was beat Caleb to within an inch of his life. A few quick steps and I had reached them. I grabbed his arm, releasing it from Natasha.

"Get away from her," my voice was harsh and threatening. Caleb stumbled back and I realized he had been drinking. "Natasha, are you okay?" I looked at her and realized that at that moment all I was looking at was a shell of the girl I'd arrived with. Her eyes had glazed over and she was shaking uncontrollably. While I had so many things I wanted to do to Caleb right at that moment, I knew it would have to wait. I took another step closer to her and gently placed my hand on her upper arm.

"Natasha, sweetheart. It's okay."

"Troy, I don't feel so good."

I pulled her tightly into my arms. I felt her trembling body beginning to relax as her arms wrapped around me.

"Shh...it's okay. I'm here," I whispered into her ear.

She clung to me and then the tears began to fall until she was on the verge of hysterical crying. I knew I needed to get her out of there, but she wasn't in any position to get in the car and I couldn't hold her while I was driving.

"Here, let's go out back okay?"

She nodded and I quickly guided her out to the back patio area where benches lined the edge. Caleb had vanished and it was probably a good thing. I sat her gently on the bench and pulled her tightly against me, letting her calm down.

"Natasha, what happened? Did he hurt you?" I asked. If he'd laid a finger on her he was going to regret it.

"I was coming back from the bathroom. I didn't see him until he had hold of my arm. He was drunk. He wanted to know why I was with you and not him. Then he said it was your fault that your sister was dead and that you were a workaholic and couldn't care about anyone but yourself. He touched my face and had hold of my arm but that was it."

"That's it. I'll be right back." I was so angry, all reasoning just fled. Right now, all I wanted to do was rearrange all the features on Caleb's smug face.

"No, Troy. Please don't leave me. He's not worth it." Natasha's grip on my arms tightened. She wasn't letting me go.

"He put his hands on you. He scared you. He's not getting away with that."

"He was drunk. I don't know what is wrong with him. He was never like this before. I told you, all last year he was super helpful with my projects. He was never threatening or mean."

"Being drunk is no excuse. He better stay clear of you."

"The program. We need to get back. I must look a wreck."

"No, I don't care about the program. I'm more worried about you. You are more important than any award. I'll just text my parents and let them know we're leaving."

"I feel bad. What if you guys win. You won't be there to get the award."

I turned her head slightly so she faced me. Her eyes were red and swollen; black was streaked down her cheeks from her mascara. "Natasha. It doesn't matter. I don't care. You were going into a full-blown panic attack and it scared me."

"Troy, how does Caleb know so much about your sister?"

So much anger and resentment came bubbling back to the surface. Emotions and feelings I'd worked so hard to shove down and bury. I knew I couldn't have this conversation here with her. It wasn't the place.

"Let's go. I'll explain everything. But not here."

I sent off a quick text to my parents letting them know that Natasha wasn't feeling well and that we were leaving.

Standing up, I held my hand out to her. She took it and held it tightly as we walked to my car in silence.

The drive back to town was quiet. The mood completely shifted from just a few hours previous. Natasha held my hand in her lap, but I could tell she had withdrawn. My heart broke and I wondered how I could bring her back out of herself.

She wanted to know more about Talise and it was probably time to tell her the rest of the story. I hadn't known until tonight how important that might be.

"Are you taking me back to the dorm?"

"Not yet. You wanted to know about Talise. We're headed to my house. I'll answer all your questions. But some things you might need to see for yourself."

"Oh. You don't have to tell me if you don't want to. It's really none of my business. I'm sorry."

"I think you do need to know. It might help you understand."

"Understand what?"

"You'll see." I turned to look at her and hoped that this was the right thing to do and that it didn't make things worse for her. But I didn't know what else to do.

CHAPTER SIXTEEN

~ *Natasha* ~

$\mathcal{T}roy$ pulled into the driveway of what I assumed was his house. He'd never brought me here before. We'd always gone out or we'd hung out at my dorm. I knew he still lived with his parents and in today's world that was smart. Living expenses were crazy expensive, and I knew he was focused on getting through his licensing exams. He still had at a couple of years of internship he had to finish along with the many written exams.

He turned off the car and I followed him up the walk to the front door. He unlocked the door and began to push it open. "You're not afraid of dogs, are you? Big dogs?" he asked.

"No, why? Is it going to eat me?" I tried to tease and lighten the mood.

"She's a sweetheart but she's also a Pit-bull and a lot of people are scared of them. If you just walk in like you own the place, she'll just follow you. Probably lick you to death more than anything."

"Okay." I knew dogs could sense fear and while I wasn't afraid of dogs, you never knew how they would react to someone new. My older brother Quinn was allergic so we'd never been able to have dogs when we were growing up.

Troy walked through the entryway and sure enough a big brown and black brindle Pit-bull was barking and wagging her tail.

"Easy Sadie, good girl," he said as he leaned down and petted her huge head.

I shut the door behind me and walked a few steps closer to Troy and his dog. I pulled my fingers in a ball and carefully put out my hand for her to smell. "Hey, girl. It's okay." Sadie proceeded to lick my hand, pushed it aside with her nose and then turn and ran to the back door.

"See, she's totally fine." He smiled as he walked towards me and locked the front door and then went to let Sadie outside.

I waited in the entry way not sure where to go. There was a large open living area directly in front of me that looked out onto the backyard. To the right was a dining area and the kitchen. The space was vaulted with wooden trusses all open to each other. Dormers facing the backyard would add nice diffused light during the day. The room was comfortable and simply decorated.

Troy turned from the back door. "Come on in. Make yourself at home. Can I get you anything to drink? Water? Soda?"

"No, I'm okay right now." I sat on the large sectional couch that faced a flat screen T.V. that was mounted over the fireplace hearth. Troy sat down next to me. Turning so he was facing me, he reached for my hands that lay in my lap. I slid off my silver heals and turned so I was facing him, one leg tucked underneath me. I could tell he was nervous, tension radiated through him.

"I don't even know where to start. I've known Caleb and his family pretty much my entire life. Caleb's dad and my dad went through architectural school together. They were good friends. As you know, I'm older, by just over three years than Caleb and Talise. Caleb is an only child. After he was born his mom had several miscarriages but was never able to carry another child full term.

"Our families did a lot of things together when we were growing up. Caleb was like a younger brother. We'd go on camping trips, we'd have sleepovers, dinners, spent holidays together, you name it. As we grew older, Caleb and Talise started dating. They were super close. They'd been doing things together for so long that the next step to a romantic relationship wasn't surprising. Their entire senior year they were together, then after graduation, something happened. Something changed.

"Caleb quit coming over, Talise just clammed up. She'd spend hours in her room by herself. She was quiet and wouldn't go out and do anything. She came to me a couple of times wanting to talk, but something was always in the way. I was headed out to meet friends, or I had a class, or a jobsite I had to go to. I was completely wrapped up in everything I was doing I couldn't even see that my own sister was falling apart.

"I had run into Caleb a couple of times during the summer and all he'd tell me was that they had an argument and things were over. That she called it off not him. That he'd tried to talk to her but she had blocked him. That he had no idea why she wasn't talking to him and that she had destroyed their relationship and broken his heart. He'd then turn things on me and ask me what I did to her, that I must have said or done something and that's why she wouldn't return his calls anymore. Our conversations never went anywhere and always ended with some pretty heated words.

"When she took the sleeping pills, every bone in my body told me that Caleb was a huge part. But I also felt guilty because I wondered if I'd just taken the extra time to listen to her would it had made a difference?

"After the funeral, there was a rift between our families. While our parents still get together on occasion, things between Caleb and myself have never been the same. We went our separate ways and stay out of each other's way. I've never trusted Caleb since. Something went horribly wrong between them and it wasn't just a normal teenager argument."

I sat there listening to Troy as he poured out the story. He was right, so many things now were falling into place. The tension between Troy and Caleb that first night at dinner right after I'd gotten the job with DeLuca Architects. I had always wondered how they knew each other.

"But why would he be so against you dating me? How does that play a part in any of it?" I asked, completely confused.

"That's how Caleb has always been. He's fiercely competitive and you were something that he wanted and he wasn't getting. Being an only child, he was spoiled. Not that it should have any importance, but he has always been used to getting what he wants. After the funeral Caleb and I got into it pretty bad. I was so angry and looking to find some sort of answers. We almost came to blows at the cemetery after the service. My dad stepped between us and broke it up. We really haven't spoken since. The couple of times I've run into him with you pretty much sums up the majority of our conversations over the last three years."

"I'm so sorry about Talise. But Troy, no matter what, you can't take the responsibility for what happened to her. She made that choice, even if you had talked to her doesn't mean anything would have changed."

"But it could have, Natasha. That's what I live with every day, is that maybe it would have made a difference."

"You can't keep living with that guilt. You don't know, and there's nothing you can do about it now."

"My parents can't even make themselves go through her room and clean it out. It looks exactly like it did three years ago when she died."

"They've never gone through anything? What if there were clues to what was going on in her things? Answers to some of your questions?"

"She had a journal like I mentioned before that was in her nightstand, but several pages were ripped out. Everything that was left wasn't anything out of the ordinary. It was all before her high school graduation. There weren't any pages from after graduation."

"Did she leave any type of suicide note?"

"No, nothing."

"So maybe it wasn't intentional?"

"Why else would she take an entire bottle of sleeping pills?"

"I don't know. I was just trying to offer some other options. I know what it feels like to not want to go through another day. You wonder if you're ever going to feel normal again. I still wonder that some days. It's not a good place to be in."

"Did you ever think about ending things?" Troy asked his eyes searched mine, sadness had crept into his features the moment he had started talking about Talise.

"No, I was never quite in that dark of a place. Justine was a huge support for me and I knew that I would get through it. Somehow, someway, but that doesn't mean that things weren't bad. Still are sometimes.

"I hate how something can snap me into a panic so quickly and I feel completely out of control. Those moments are lessening, but still happen. Tonight, I think it was because I felt cornered by Caleb. I don't think he would have hurt me, but there was a moment when I wasn't sure.

"I knew the alcohol wasn't helping the situation, but I felt helpless, like things were moving in slow motion and there wasn't anything I could do to stop them."

"Come here. I'm so sorry."

I crawled practically in Troy's lap and snuggled into his warm chest and held him tightly. His fingers brushed back my hair from my face as he held me. We sat wrapped in each other's arms in silence; for how long I didn't know. My eyes still burned from the tears earlier and I hadn't even braved looking at myself in the mirror. I was likely a complete and utter mess.

Leaning back, I looked into his eyes. My hands now rested on either side of his neck, resting on his shoulders. I leaned forward, my lips lightly touching his. His lips were warm and soft as he kissed me back. I felt his hands reach further around me settling on my hips, pulling me closer. He deepened the kiss, his tongue seeking entry. I sighed as I let myself go, to be caught up in the feelings that he was stirring inside. The pit of my stomach ached and I couldn't get enough of him.

My hands found their way around his neck, interlocking, holding him to me. Heat began to build inside of me and I pushed closer to him, trying to find some relief. I felt his tongue retreat and he slowly pulled away, his breathing was heavy as he leaned his forehead against mine and he kissed the tip of my nose.

"I'm not going to be able to stop if we keep this up right now. And I really don't think you're ready for things to go any further right at this moment. I want to make sure that you are ready." He sighed as he pulled back, his hands resting on the sides of my cheeks.

"You're right. I'm sorry I started anything." I searched his eyes for any sign of regret or pity, but there was none. I only saw concern.

"Come here." He leaned back against the couch, his feet propped up on the ottoman and he pulled me alongside of him. His arm rested along mine as I stretched out next to him. My head lay over his heart, while my right arm slid behind his back as my left hand rested on his chest. His head leaned against mine. I could have laid there like that forever.

~ *Troy* ~

Natasha's even breathing indicated she had drifted off to sleep. I'm sure the adrenaline burst that she had earlier probably had left her exhausted. My thoughts were all over the place trying to figure out what Caleb's angle was with Natasha. I'd never really seen that more violent side to him, but I also hadn't been around him very often when he was drinking and that likely was the difference. It made me wonder though if Talise had been with him when he was drinking and maybe that was what they had argued over. He definitely was a different person with alcohol racing through him, and not in a good way.

I thought about what Natasha had said about clues in her things. After Talise was gone, it was hard for any of us to go into her room. Everything was just as she left it. Could there be clues to what she had been going through still in her room? I was curious now and knew I needed to go through her things.

My phone vibrated in my pocket and I pulled it out. It was a message from my mom, a picture of the team at the awards ceremony. We had indeed won not one, but both awards that we'd been nominated for. She asked how Natasha was feeling and to let me know everyone was going out to celebrate after if we wanted to join them. I sent a quick text back letting her know that we'd pass tonight. I slid it back in my pocket just as Natasha stirred.

"Was I sleeping?" she asked as she lifted her head and looked up at me groggily.

"For a little bit. Not super long. Your body must have needed it."

"Where's the bathroom?"

"Down the hall, second door on the left."

"Thanks, I'll be right back."

Sadie was whining at the back door so I walked over and let her back in. Her tail was wagging back and forth with such force it was like a whip in the air. We'd had her since she was six weeks old, now close to a hundred pounds she still thought she was the size of a lap dog. She followed me back to the couch and proceeded to jump up laying her head in my lap while we waited for Natasha to return.

When Natasha returned her face was cleared of the streaks of black that had stained her cheeks.

"Why didn't you tell me how awful I looked?" she asked as she sat next to me.

"You never looked awful. It was just makeup. It was temporary." I smiled as I put my arm around her shoulders and brought her close to me. "Do you feel better?"

"Yes, a bit," she replied as she patted Sadie's head. The dog's tail thumped in approval.

"She's so pretty. I love the little bit of white on her chest," Natasha commented as she continued to stroke Sadie's ears and top of her head.

"She's a good dog. She used to be Talise's constant companion. She always slept on Talise's bed with her. Even after Talise was gone, she'd lay on her bed for months. It was heartbreaking. She sleeps with me now most of the time. Her favorite place to sleep is on top of the pillows at your head. Talise let her sleep that way when she was a puppy. Which was cool when Sadie was the size of a cat, but at almost a hundred pounds now it's not so cute." I smiled as I rubbed behind Sadie's ears.

"Have you heard anything about the awards?" Natasha asked.

"Yeah. We won."

Natasha sat up and looked at me. "Really? That's awesome Troy! You guys worked hard on those. I'm so sorry you weren't there to see it."

"It's okay. You are way more important than any award ceremony."

She smiled and leaned over brushing my lips with a light kiss. "You're such a charmer."

I laughed. That wasn't what I was expecting to hear from her at that moment. I leaned back against the couch. "So, I was thinking while you were sleeping."

"Um, thinking, huh? That could be a bit dangerous," she teased.

"Ha, ha. Well, a couple things that you said about Talise made me start to wonder. Neither my parents nor I, have really been through all of her stuff. My mom is still in denial sometimes and can't bring herself to pack up all of Talise's things. If everything is just how it was, then there's this illusion that she's coming back. Would you be willing to help me go through her room? I'm not sure I can do it by myself and you might see something that I'd miss because you don't really know her or what you're looking for."

"Of course, if that's what you want. I'll help. Just tell me when. It's the least I can do."

"How about now?"

"Now?"

"Yeah, why not. If there's nothing there, then we've lost nothing. But what if there is some sort of clue in her things?"

"Okay."

I stood up and offered her my hand. She took it and I gently pulled her up. "Thank you."

"There's no need to thank me."

Guiding her down the hall, with her hand in mine, I really hoped this wasn't a bad idea. I was starting to stress out a little bit wondering how my parents would feel if they came home while we were going through Talise's things.

While I wanted to find answers, part of me was scared at what I might find. Was there a darker side to

Talise that no one knew about that she had kept hidden and buried from all of us?

We reached her closed door, I let Natasha's hand go while I turned the knob and pushed the door open. I flipped on the overhead ceiling fan light and looked around the room like I'd just stepped back in time. My mom hadn't even moved the sweater that Talise had tossed carelessly on the back of her desk chair.

Her laptop still sat closed on the desk just like Talise had left it. I knew the only time anyone was in here was when our housekeepers came, they would dust and vacuum and that was it.

Natasha stood at the door entrance and I wondered what she was thinking as she looked around the room. "Well, where should we start?" I asked her.

CHAPTER SEVENTEEN

~ *Natasha* ~

I couldn't believe how preserved Talise's room was. When Troy had said that it was pretty much exactly how she'd left it, he wasn't kidding. It was a bit eerie, like she could walk through the door at any minute.

The walls were painted light gray with the wall behind her bed accented with six wide white and gray stripes. Her full-size bed sat pushed up against the accent wall. The furniture in the room was all white, which contrasted with the gray, light pink and teal accents found throughout the room. The space was comfortable and cozy, and I felt like an intruder. Maybe this wasn't such a great idea.

Troy stood in the middle of the room at the foot of the bed. There was a white cushioned bench at the end of the bed with a pale pink fuzzy blanket folded over the edge. Sadie had followed us into the room. She walked over to the bed, jumped up, and turned in several circles before finally sprawling out at the end of the bed. Her head resting between her front paws as they hung over the edge of the mattress.

I forced my legs to move, and walked over to Troy. He was sitting on the mattress next to Sadie. I sat next to him, closest to the head of the bed.

"Where did you find her journal?" I asked him quietly.

"She had it under some books in the nightstand. In the top drawer. We did look through her nightstand and also her desk and computer, but we didn't really come across anything."

"What about her phone or did she have any type of tablet like an iPad?"

"We went through her phone, text messages, notes, photos, but nothing on there that we thought was informative."

"Did you keep her phone?"

"I think it's still in her nightstand drawer where we left it. We'd have to charge it. Should I go get a charger?"

"If you don't think there's anything of value on it, then let's not focus on that right now."

"She did have an iPad, and to be honest I don't remember looking through that as thoroughly."

"Did she have any type of notebooks, scrapbooks, or places she would store keepsakes?"

"I don't really remember any of those."

"Okay, well let's start looking."

I opened up the nightstand drawer and pulled out the contents. Troy moved to Talise's desk and booted up her computer and started going through her desk drawers. Just like Troy had said her phone and journal were in the top drawer, along with a couple of romance novels, a few pens, a polaroid camera with extra film, nail polish, hair ties, and other random stuff.

Her journal burned in my hands as I held it. Knowing that inside was personal thoughts and feelings of a girl I never knew. I felt like I was intruding into her soul as I flipped open the pages. Talise's handwriting was neat and frilly, entries written in different color inks. The first entry had been almost two years before she died. I flipped through the pages, catching little glimpses into her past. Like Troy had said there didn't seem to be anything that stood out, it was mostly normal events in the daily life of a teenage high school student.

Near the end it was obvious there had been several pages ripped from the book. Fragments of paper still caught in the spine. I wondered if she really had trashed the pages or were they hidden somewhere. Thoughts of something too painful that she couldn't deal with. Maybe she thought it was easier to remove them, but held onto them because she couldn't quite get herself to throw them out? It would have been something I'd have done.

There had been many times I'd thought about writing about what had happened to me, but ultimately, I didn't want to see the words on paper. At that moment in time, for me at least, it was easier to deal with it if I didn't see the words. Writing the words down made them more real and vivid in my brain, and I hadn't been in a place that I thought I could handle that.

Her last few entries were just days before she passed were vague and nothing out of the normal. Nothing that would foreshadow what would happen. No wonder Troy and his parents were baffled.

I placed the loose items back in the drawer where I'd found them. Opening the door underneath I flipped through the books that were lined up on the shelves. All typical high school reading, many of them I'd read myself.

I went to the end of the bed and inspected the white bench that was located at the foot. I knew many benches where the seat lifted up and you could store extra blankets, or other things. I had one myself back home that I kept items in. The cushion flipped up and inside was mostly empty. The space inside wasn't very deep so storage was limited, but there was a soft fuzzy blanket stored inside.

Troy had pulled out stacks of loose papers and items from the desk drawers and was sorting them on the desk. There was a dresser on the adjacent wall with a flat screen TV sitting on top. I opened each drawer, carefully pulling out clothing items to see if anything had been stashed in the drawers. It was really like she was still alive.

I felt like we were going to get caught at any minute with her walking in the room wondering what in the world we were doing rummaging through her things. I made sure to neatly fold each item back up and replace it where I had found it.

Her closet had mirrored sliding doors and I slid one of the doors open, exposing clothes neatly hung on a double rod. She had been organized that's for sure. Short sleeve tops hung from the top rod while long sleeves were on the bottom. She had organized them by color.

I moved them around looking to see if there was anything on the floor or any boxes stored, but found nothing. Shoes were lined up on the floor and on a short shelf. Tennis shoes, flats, boots, heals, a pair of pink fuzzy slippers where the only thing slightly askew.

I slid the doors to allow access to the other side of the closet. Here there was only one rod, which allowed extra length for dresses or anything that needed more room to hang. Her shoes continued on this side, but they were in boxes stacked one on top of each other.

A HEALING TOUCH

Crumpled fabric caught my eye in the back corner of the closet. I kneeled on the floor and pulled several shoeboxes out of the way. Sure enough, shoved all the way in the back of the closet in the far corner was a ball of rumpled clothes.

I pulled them out so that I could look at them closer. Shaking out the wrinkles in the top I held it in front of me to inspect it. It was a mint green with gray sleeves, baseball three-quarter sleeved t-shirt. The neckline though was stretched out and had a slight rip. Under the t-shirt was a pair of jeans. I shook them out and laid them flat on the carpet. I couldn't see anything unusual about them. But it was odd, why were these clothes crumpled in her closet when there was a clothing hamper siting right next to her closet?

Standing up I pushed her few dresses all the way to the side, out of the way so I could see better in the back corner of the closet. There was something else in the corner but I couldn't tell what it was. I got back down on my knees. My dress made it difficult to move much, but I was able to crawl back a little further into the closet so that I could reach the back corner.

My fingers touched satin and every bone in my body knew they were undergarments. I carefully pulled them out, almost afraid to see what I held. Sure enough, it was a matching set of gray satin and lace, boy short panties and bra. I placed them both on the floor next to the jeans. In the better light I realized that there was good size rip in the side of the panties.

I sat there stunned, fear, and a sick feeling in my stomach. Images of that morning I had woken up missing my underwear and not knowing where I was were running through my head. I had wanted to burn the clothing that I'd been wearing, but the police had kept it just in case they were able to find any evidence on it.

Maybe, I was just making more out of it that it seemed. Maybe, there was something special about these clothes that Talise had wanted to keep, for good memories and I was just superimposing my own negative thoughts.

But if they had been for a good special reason, why were they all crumpled up? Neglected in the back corner of her closet.

My thoughts were running wild, I was so focused on the clothes that were laid in front of me that I never heard Troy get up. His hand on my shoulder startled me, pulling me out of my head.

"Are you okay?" he asked me, concern was evident in his voice.

I looked up into his worried face. "I'm not sure."

"What did you find? It just looks like an outfit."

"I found it crumpled in the back of the closet. Troy, everything else in her drawers, and her closet is hung and folded perfect. So why, is there a crumpled outfit, including her underwear tossed in the corner of her closet? And look, see the neckline on the top, it has a slight tear where the neckline was sewn and the lace on her panties is ripped."

"You're right. Wait a second, there's something familiar about that outfit."

Troy walked back over to the computer and started pulling up the photo library, scrolling through pictures.

"I knew it looked familiar. Here, come look."

Pushing myself up off the floor I walked over and stood behind Troy as he sat in front of the computer. My heart almost stopped. There on the screen was a smiling Talise, wearing the exact outfit that was on the floor, wrapped in a side hug with Caleb.

"Natasha, this picture was taken the night of the graduation party that they went to. This is the last picture of the two of them together."

"Are you serious?"

"Yes, look at the date on the image. And I remember that night, I had told Talise if things got crazy at the party that I'd come get her, no questions asked. I was up late that night studying for finals. I remember when she came home, she didn't pop her head in to say hi, which she always did. I just figured she was tired and exhausted since it was super late.

"She shut her door that night too which she didn't usually do at night. I woke up the next morning to Sadie whining to get out of her room so she could go outside to the bathroom. Until this very minute, I never had thought much about it. Do you think something happened that night at the party?"

"Right now, everything is pointing in that direction. You were the one that said you saw a change in her right after that party. Now this? Her and Caleb breaking up right after? Why? Something had to have happened that night. You know if Caleb was at all responsible or somehow a part of what happened he's never going to say anything. What about her friends? Was there anyone else there that you could ask questions?"

"I know most of her friends were there at the party. I guess I can reach out to them. Some of them are still in the area, while others are away at different colleges."

"It's worth a shot. I would have thought though if they had seen or suspected anything odd that they would have reached out to your family after she died."

My hands rested on his shoulders, as I peered over at the pictures on the screen. It was odd seeing Caleb standing there with his arms wrapped around Talise. She looked so happy. Her long hair was a dark reddish brown, her skin light, and her green eyes a striking emerald color. Her nose and cheeks were sprinkled with freckles. I could see a lot of Camille in her facial structure. Caleb was smiling, a full, almost content smile. While he looked the same, there was something different about him now. Not as carefree maybe, it was hard to pinpoint the difference.

"Probably. Was there anything else in the closet that was odd?" Troy asked as he turned in his chair to face me.

"I wasn't finished looking through that side. I had just opened the doors when the clothes caught my eye in the corner."

Troy stood up and I followed him over to the closet where the rumpled clothes still lay on the floor. Hiking my dress above my knees, I kneeled down so I could search the bottom of Talise's closet. I pulled out the several boxes of shoes, but there was nothing else laying loose on the floor.

Troy was pulling down the few boxes that were stacked on the upper shelf above the hanging rod. Each one he carried over to the bed. While he went through those boxes, I started opening the shoeboxes. Every box I opened appeared to have been Talise's special occasion shoes. They were mostly heels or satin ballet flats with minimal wear. The last box I opened was a pair of gray Vans. Completely out of context compared to the rest of the shoes I'd opened. I tilted the box to look closer and was even more confused that the box wasn't even a Vans shoebox.

It didn't make any sense. All the rest of her casual shoes, flip flops, flats, tennis shoes, sandals, slippers were on the other side of the closet and all loose. They were just sitting on the floor or the shelf. Not a single pair were left in boxes. Why was this pair kept away in a box?

I pulled each shoe out and examined them. They looked practically brand new; they couldn't have been worn more than a couple of times. I set them beside me and then picked the box up and my heart stopped. At the bottom of the box were folded pieces of paper. Carefully, I pulled them out and unfolded them. My hands started to shake and I realized that I was holding the ripped-out pages from Talise's journal.

"Troy."

"There's nothing in these boxes but old school papers, and crafts from when she was a kid."

"Troy, I think I found them."

"Found what?" He asked as he crouched behind me.

I held out the papers I was holding. "Her missing journal pages."

"What?! Are you serious?"

"I'm pretty sure. I didn't read them. I don't think it's my place to do that. You should read them first."

"Where did you find these?"

"They were on the bottom of a shoe box, with these shoes on top. All the rest of her shoes in the boxes are dressy shoes. Except these." I held the Vans up for him to see.

"I can't believe you found them." His voice was almost a whisper. I knew he was probably in as much shock as I was right now.

He stood up and offered me his hand. I grabbed it, pulling myself up off the floor and followed him to the bench at the foot of the bed where he sat down. I sat next to him, my arm wrapped around his waist and my head leaned against his shoulder. Letting him know I was there for support.

"I'm kind of scared Natasha. I want the answers, but do I? What if there's more in here that I don't want to know?"

"Is it better to know why, than to always wonder? No matter what the answer is? At least you'll have some sort of closure. We don't even know yet what she wrote down. There may not be any answers in those pages, but more questions you might not ever find answers to."

~ *Troy* ~

Staring down at the pages I held in my hand, it felt like they were on fire. I swear I could feel heat radiating through the loose sheets. Hold them too tightly and they would burn. I was stunned that Natasha had found them, and was still trying to wrap my head around the fact that for the past couple of years, these pages were just sitting here in her closet. They could have so easily been thrown out and we'd never have found them. So many times, I'd begged my mom to go through her things and donate them. But she refused to listen to me and everything sat just as it had been the last time Talise was in this room.

Unfolding the pages, I looked at the date on the top of the first page and knew it was the morning after the graduation party. My heart was pounding so hard it felt like it was ready to burst from my chest. I started reading the words out loud. I didn't know what I was going to find or discover, but I felt that Natasha deserved to hear it at the same time I did.

June 15

I sit here and can't believe how someone that I thought I loved could turn on me and hurt me. After all these years. Why? Why would Caleb have destroyed all trust that I had in him? I have no more tears. I think I've shed them all. Sadie is just laying next to me. her head laying on my stomach. I know she feels my pain and my heart shattering. I knew he'd had too much to drink. I'd never seen him that drunk before. He was an entirely different person that night. someone I didn't know or recognize.

We had been in the game room playing pool with several of our classmates. I left to go to the bathroom and Caleb followed. We were laughing and holding hands. He locked the door behind us and reached for me. We were kissing. and making out. I knew I'd had too much to drink. I was starting to feel sick. I wasn't used to drinking and the alcohol was catching up to me quickly. His hand reached for my jeans and he had them unzipped and was pushing them down.

Melissa A. Hanson

I was overwhelmed with the burning inside me. The need deep inside. but I wasn't ready for this right now. My thoughts were foggy. I was getting dizzy. He was kissing me again. I could feel his need and I was out of breath. I looked up at him and asked him to slow down. To stop. But then everything went dark.

I woke up in a bed. it was still dark out. I couldn't make out the shapes in the room. everything was spinning and I thought I was going to throw up everything I'd had for dinner. I could feel my shirt being lifted off me but I fought to push it back down. I thought I heard it ripping. I struggled to get up. but I felt pinned down. My voice didn't even sound like it was my own. I tried to tell him to stop. I wasn't ready. It was like I was talking to a stranger. How could my sweet Caleb be doing this to me? I felt like I disconnected from my body.

He didn't speak. but held my hands tight in one hand while his other hand had unzipped my jeans and I could feel them being pulled down. My panties stretching until they finally gave way. The ripping pain as he drove himself into me caused me to cry out. only to have my mouth covered as I struggled to breath. This could not be happening right now. This was not how I imagined my first time.

I struggled to break free of his grasp but even as drunk as he was he was too strong for me. I laid there as tears streamed down my face. I lost track of time and then it was over and he was gone. I was stunned, shocked. This boy I'd known all my life was not who I thought he was. Where did this monster come from? How could I have been so delusional?

I pulled my panties and jeans back up. I was scared to leave the room. I'm not sure how long I laid there with my knees pulled up to my chest crying. I had to get out of there. I needed to get home before anyone saw me.

Rage burned through every bone in my body as I read her words. I wanted to tear Caleb apart from limb to limb.

"I fucking knew it. I knew Caleb did something to her. And now I have the proof," I hissed. I was so angry I was shaking.

"I'm so sorry, Troy." Natasha's arm tightened around my waist.

I looked down at her as she sat next to me and I realized in that minute what she must be reliving in her mind as well. "I'm sorry Natasha, I know hearing that probably just brought back a lot of feelings that you didn't want to relive."

She looked up at me, her eyes glistening with tears. "As bad as things were for me, maybe not having specific memories of what happened is better. Talise looked into the face of someone she knew. Someone she trusted and loved and was betrayed in every way possible. I know how dirty and disgusted I felt afterwards. I can't even imagine how she felt."

"I can't believe she didn't say anything."

"Really? I can. It's a horrible feeling. You want it all to go away. You don't want to think about it. You want to shove it down so far that it never resurfaces. You don't feel like yourself. I still don't some days. A part of me was taken that night and I'll never get it back. I'm sure Talise had similar feelings. Hers were probably way worse than even what I went through. It's a delicate situation. Even if she had come forward and said something, your family would have believed her, but ultimately it would have been her word against his. How do you prove it? They were both eighteen at the time. Think about the position she was in."

I pulled Natasha tighter to me. I knew she was right, but it still didn't sit right with me. Caleb wasn't getting away with this. I wasn't going to let him. I knew there was something so familiar about Natasha and now the pieces were falling into place. I saw many of the same signs with Talise, but I never really asked Talise if she was okay. I never sat down and talked to her when I could see she was struggling, and I wasn't sure if I'd ever be able to forgive myself for that. My little sister was gone and I wondered if I had just done things differently would she still be here?

"Is there anything else after that entry?" Natasha asked.

Flipping through the loose sheets that I held in my hand I realized there were several more entries and a black and white photo that slipped out of my hands and landed on the floor. I reached down and picked the photo off the ground and I started to shake even worse.

It couldn't be. But it was. Talise's name was typed in bright white letters at the top of the picture.

"What? Troy, what is it?" Natasha asked as she leaned over to get a better look.

"She was pregnant Natasha." My hands were shaking as I handed her the glossy image of an ultrasound.

"No way. But didn't they say anything when they did her autopsy?" She asked as she took the photo from me.

"No, they never said anything about her being pregnant. How could she have taken the sleeping pills if she knew she was pregnant? Why didn't she say anything to us?"

"Finish her journal, maybe there's more information in there," Natasha urged as I felt her tighten her hold around my waist.

August 2

My suspicions and worst nightmare is true. I took six different tests and every damn one of them came back positive. How can this be happening to me? I just wanted to put that night behind me and pretend it had never happened.

Caleb keeps trying to contact me. He keeps asking me what happened. Where I went, and why I won't talk to him. I can't believe him. Seriously? How can he even ask me those things? He keeps telling me he put me in the bedroom after I passed out in the bathroom on him. And when he came back up to check on me and take me home that I was gone. But I don't believe him. I know he was drunk that night but I don't think he was that drunk to not remember. I blocked his number. I don't care if I ever see him again.

But what am I going to do now? I can't have a baby right now and knowing how it was conceived. Would I ever get over that? I'm supposed to start college in just a few weeks. What am I going to do? I know my parents and Troy too are wondering what's wrong with me. They keep asking what happened with Caleb, but I can't tell them. I can't get the words out. I just keep telling them we broke up and to leave it alone.

August 18

I finally made myself go to the woman's clinic today. My mom has been watching me like a hawk the last few days. I think she knows something is wrong with me. I just kept telling her I wasn't feeling good. She told me if I wasn't feeling better soon that she was going to take me to urgent care. I told her I'd go to the doctor myself but I didn't tell her what doctor. They confirmed that I am pregnant. They even did an ultrasound. Why I took the picture with me I'll never know. Maybe someday I'll get the guts to tell Caleb. But I'm not letting him have any say in what I do with my body. He doesn't have any right.

A HEALING TOUCH

I go back tomorrow. I didn't realize that I wouldn't have to have surgery. That just a couple of pills and this whole nightmare will be over. If I'd been thinking clearly after that night at the party I should have just gotten a morning after pill, but I didn't even think about pregnancy. And now here I am. I don't know if this is the best thing for me right now, but I can't be pregnant.

My parents will be gone this weekend so the timing is good. They will never need to know. I will only need to worry about Troy being around. But I know he's been busy with summer school and spends a lot of time at school on the weekends so hopefully he won't notice.

The nurse told me I had to have a driver come with me. I asked her if it was ok to have an Uber driver. She was hesitant. She said it was better if I had a friend or family member to be with me for support. But that would mean I'd have to tell someone and I don't want anyone knowing. Not even my friends. I know they would be here to support me, but I don't want all the questions. And then I'd have to tell them what happened and I just want it all to go away. If I don't tell anyone that means no one will know and I can put this all in my past.

If I'm honest with myself. I'm scared. things can go wrong. they made sure that I understood all the different scenarios. That there was still a chance the pills wouldn't work and that I'd still need to have a surgical procedure. I just want it over with.

August 20

I want to die. I've never been in so much pain in my life. The cramping started a few hours after I got home from the clinic. I was so glad that my Uber driver was a woman. When she dropped me off she asked how I was getting home. I told her I'd call for another ride and she said not to worry. that she'd stay and wait for me. She was an older lady and she kept asking me if I was ok and wanted to make sure there was someone at home to take care of me. Of course. I lied to her and told her I was fine and that someone would be home soon. I could see was worried when she dropped me off. Sadie hasn't left my side. I know she senses I'm in pain.

My parents left as scheduled and the house is quiet. Troy has come in and out a few times but so far. I've been able to avoid running into him. I had a close call though running into Troy. I thought he wasn't going to leave. I hurt so bad. The cramping had gotten so intense. I was running to the bathroom just as another cramp was gripping my stomach. I wanted to scream it was so intense. Troy was coming down the hall from his room. And he saw me. he immediately knew something was wrong with me and kept asking me a million questions. Finally he gave up when I told him I ate something bad and if he didn't move out of the way I was going to throw up all over him. He finally moved but said he was going to stay and make sure I didn't need anything. I kept telling him to go. not worry about me. I was a big girl and just ate something bad. I'd be fine no need for him to stay. He finally left and I barely made it to the bathroom in time.

Sitting on the toilet the blood gushed from me. I had to bite into the sleeve of my shirt to keep from crying out. Tears streamed down my face. I'm not sure how long I spent in the bathroom. after a while I just laid on the floor. Sadie whining at the door to get in. I pushed myself on my knees and crawled to the door and opened it for her. I couldn't bear to look at the toilet as I flushed it. all I could see was red. The pain is finally starting to lift. the bleeding hasn't stopped though. a constant reminder.

September 6
I can't sleep. I'm so exhausted. the bags under my eyes are getting harder and harder to conceal. I've tried everything. Why can't I sleep? Every time I lay down my mind doesn't shut down and so many things keep running through it. I wonder if I did the right thing by getting rid

of the pregnancy. I'm so conflicted. but it's over and I can't change anything now.

My hate builds daily towards Caleb. I've run into him a couple times and all I feel is disgust. How could I have loved him. and trusted him? Everyone is asking me questions. They know something is wrong. I don't know who to talk to. I tried reaching out to Troy. but he's busy and I'm not sure if I could even talk to him even if he had a minute. Several of my friends have already left for college. they don't understand what happened with Caleb. I just tell them he was a high school romance and it's time to move on. But I know they aren't buying that. I start my freshman year in just a few weeks. but if I can't get any sleep how am I going to be able to focus? I feel like I'm a walking zombie.

September 10
I finally had my first night of good sleep. I gave up and went to the doctor and got a prescription for sleeping pills. I feel better today. For the first time in months. I kind of feel like myself again. I know I have to be careful with the pills.

The doctor wants to see me back in a month to re-evaluate. She made it very clear that this is not a long-term solution. She suggested that I find a therapist to *talk to and work on self-relaxing techniques and trying to resolve the issues that are keeping my brain from not letting itself shut down and rest. I know she's right. but it really felt so good to actually sleep. A deep sleep with no dreams. and no nightmares to wake me.*

I flipped to the next page and there was nothing. "That's it, how can that be it?" I asked. "I'm even more confused now. It sounded like she was finally starting to work things out, so why end things?"

"Maybe it wasn't intentional. What if it was an accidental overdose?"

"I still can't believe she went through all of that and never said anything to anyone? Why keep the notes, and the clothes?"

"Maybe she was starting to put it behind her and it was easier to just rip those pages out. But she couldn't quite totally get rid of them, so instead she tucked them away. Who knows, she might have even forgotten the clothes were tossed in the corner of the closet."

"I guess. I just don't know what to believe or what to do, except tear Caleb apart. Ultimately this is all his fault. He's not getting away with this."

"What are you going to do?"

"I'm not sure yet."

Natasha leaned her head against my shoulder. "I'm sorry that all this happened to Talise, but maybe find some peace, that maybe she didn't actually take her own life on purpose. That it was just an accident. A night of tossing and turning, and her brain running through so many things that she just wanted to find a way to block them out and get a good night sleep."

I sat there and absorbed the scenario that Natasha had just run through and it was plausible. Especially in hindsight now knowing a little more of what she had been going through in the weeks before her death. More pieces of the puzzle had been put into place.

Sadie sat up on Talise's bed, her ears perked up and her tail started wagging. I knew my parents were home. The thumping got louder as I heard the door from the garage slam shut and the alarm chime beep.

My mom was the first one to appear in the doorway. "Troy, what are you guys doing in here?" she asked.

"We were searching for answers." I didn't know how my parents were going to take the news of what we had found.

Mom took a few steps into the room. Her eyes sweeping the room before settling back on Natasha and I. My dad was leaning against the doorframe, the smile that had been on his face a minute before vanishing.

"We found her missing journal pages," I explained and held them out.

"What?" My mom's voice was a whisper, her face turned white as a sheet. My dad was by her side in a second, his arm tight around her waist.

"How? Where?" my dad asked.

"In her closet, in a shoebox. There are some other things too. I'm not sure how to even tell you."

"Just spit it out Troy," my dad said as he took the pages carefully from my outstretched hand.

It was close to two in the morning. My parents had finally headed to bed. My mom was pretty shaken up and my dad had been ready to get back in his car and find Caleb to confront him. In the end they calmed down enough to realize that they needed to wait and get some additional legal advice before doing anything.

Natasha was exhausted. She was struggling to keep her eyes open and I knew I needed to get her back to her dorm. We had moved from Talise's room into the living room after we had shown my parents everything we'd found. Natasha was curled up next to me on the couch, her head resting on my shoulder.

"You ready for me to take you back to your dorm?" I asked her.

"Yeah, it's been a long night."

"I know. I'm sorry. It wasn't how I'd wanted the evening to go."

"It's okay. As emotionally draining as it was for me, I know it was a hundred times worse for you and your parents. I'm really sorry, Troy. But maybe now you guys can get some closure."

Standing up, I reached my hand out for her to grab. Her hand interlocked with mine and I felt the intensity of our connection. I pulled her gently up from the couch and steadied her while she slipped her heals back on. Sadie had been laying at Natasha's feet and she followed us to the door, her tail wagging. Natasha leaned over and petted her head, scratching her behind her ears in farewell. I was in awe a little bit of how quickly Sadie had seemed to attach herself to Natasha. She was always friendly with guests we had come over, but this was different.

The drive back to the dorm was quick, the streets empty at the late hour. The wind had picked up and the temperature had dropped. According to the weather reports rain was on its way. My right hand was interlaced with Natasha's as it rested on her thigh. Her head was resting against the back of the headrest, her eyes closed. Streetlights filtered over her features as we drove through the quiet city.

She looked so peaceful, and beautiful. I knew I was falling for her, and falling hard. I wasn't sure though how ready she was for any type of serious relationship. But she was worth the wait. I knew that the road ahead was likely going to be bumpy. The reality of it was that she was still dealing with everything that had happened to her, and there was always a possibility that she might not ever totally get over it.

CHAPTER EIGHTEEN

~ *Natasha* ~

Troy was calling my name. I knew that, but I was so tired. Opening my eyes took effort and I just wanted to sleep.

"Natasha, we're back at the dorm."

"M'mk."

Troy chuckled. "Come on, let's get you inside and then you can sleep until your hearts content."

I grabbed my clutch and opened the door. Troy had already come around the car and was standing at the door waiting to help me out. I couldn't stop yawning and was looking forward to crawling into my comfy pj's and into my bed. Troy shut the door and locked his car as we walked toward the dorm. His arm was wrapped around my waist and I was leaning into him for warmth and support.

This was not how I had expected the night to go. There were so many things running through my head. I couldn't believe we'd actually found Talise's missing journal pages and my heart broke for her. To have gone through everything she had, and done it completely alone, must have been devastating. She'd never said anything to anyone.

As much as I had thought I wanted to keep everything a secret that had happened to me, I was glad that I had friends who were there for me, and that I had opened up and told them. While it hadn't taken away the pain, sharing it with them had helped. I knew that no matter what I could talk to them about anything and they would be there for me. No judgment, only support and I couldn't have asked for anything more.

Even Troy, who I hadn't expected to be so understanding, had been such a huge help in my healing. I knew I still had a long way to go, but I was determined to get my life back.

We reached my dorm room, and I pulled my keys out being as quiet as I could so I wouldn't wake up Justine. Before I unlocked the door, I reached up, and wrapped my arms around Troy's neck. His head tilted and our lips brushed, the kiss deepened quickly, melting into each other. His hands resting on my hips pulled me tighter to his chest. My body fit within his frame like it had been molded to him. I could stand here all night kissing him, but I knew I needed to get some sleep and let him get home. But I didn't want him to go.

The kiss ended and I leaned my head against his chest, my ear over his heart, I could hear his heart beat, strong and steady. His arms tight around me. Mine wrapped around his back.

"I better let you go. I'm so sorry about tonight," I whispered against his chest.

I felt his fingers lifting my chin to look up at him. "Don't be sorry. None of this is your fault."

Troy's eyes were a dark gray tonight, fitting for the crazy turmoil we'd just been through. I didn't know what to say. I wanted to tell him how much I was falling for him, but I couldn't get the words past my lips. I was so scared, scared of being hurt. Wondering was I really ready for any type of romantic relationship. Would I even be able to handle it right now?

He kissed my forehead and I hugged him one last time before unlocking the door to my dorm room. I quietly pushed the door open so that I wouldn't wake up Justine. But the dim light from the hall revealed that my dorm room was empty. At this late of hour, Justine must have stayed with her boyfriend, and right now I was kind of glad.

Turning to face him, I held out my hand. "Justine isn't here. Will you stay here with me tonight? Nothing physical, but just hold me?"

Troy took my hand and followed me into my room. There had only been one other time he'd stayed here with me weeks ago. I thought about how comfortable and safe I'd felt sleeping in his arms that night and I knew I needed that tonight. I needed to feel safe and not alone.

Flipping on the lights now that I knew that Justine wasn't here, I locked the door behind us.

"I'm going to change into something more comfortable."

"I like the sound of that." Troy teased as he pulled his suit jacket off, tossing it over the back of my desk chair.

"Yeah, I bet you do," I laughed, after the heaviness of the night it was nice to lighten the mood.

I opened my dresser drawer and pulled out leggings and my go-to oversized t-shirt. My heart was starting to race faster. I knew that Troy wouldn't try anything that I wasn't ready for. I knew I was safe, but this wasn't something that I did every day and I was still nervous.

"I'll be right back," I told him as I took my change of clothes into the adjoining bathroom.

Brushing my teeth and pulling my hair up into a ponytail, I stared at the reflection in the mirror. The face that stared back at me was my own but it wasn't. I wasn't the innocent girl I'd been just a few short months ago. But I felt stronger now. More determined that I wasn't going to let what had happened to me ruin my life or pull me down. It was in the past, dead, gone and buried. I knew that I would likely never know who had been the one to take my innocence. But I also knew that if I was to overcome this hurdle in my life, I couldn't let the fear drive me, because then he would win.

Troy was sitting on my bed when I came out of the bathroom. His shoes were off and his shirt sleeves were rolled up. He looked almost as tired as I did. I flipped off the light, plunging the room into darkness. I could still faintly see his outline as I waited for my eyes to adjust. I walked slowly to the bed. I felt his outstretched hand before I saw it. I placed my hand into his and he gently pulled me to him.

"Come on, you're exhausted." His deep voice soothed me.

He stood up as I pulled the covers back. He climbed in first, lying on his side with his back against the outside wall of the room. He patted the bed in front of him, and I slid in, my back against the front of him. He pulled the covers over us and his arm wrapped around my waist, pulling me tightly against him. His warm breath was against my neck. I ached in the pit of my stomach and my heart was racing. My exhaustion was quickly leaving and I wondered if I'd be able to calm myself down and actually get some sleep.

"Good night, Natasha."

A HEALING TOUCH

"Good night, Troy."

The heat between us was building. His arm held me snug, my body fit perfect against his every curve. I concentrated on my breathing, trying to get my brain to calm down so I could fall asleep. My heart was finally starting to slow and exhaustion was quickly pulling me into a deep sleep.

~ *Troy* ~

Holding Natasha tightly against me, my mind was racing through the events of the evening. As exhausted as I was, sleep avoided me. So many scenarios, so many things left unanswered. What happened to Talise in those final days, her final hours? Was it really intentional or was it just an accident?

I wanted to confront Caleb. Knowing he'd hurt Talise was infuriating. We grew up together. He was supposed to protect her, not hurt her. And Natasha, was it just a freak coincidence that she had been hurt as well? Could it have been Caleb, too? There was no way, right? But his recent behavior toward Natasha was off. Natasha said they'd never dated, only talked at school. So why had he all of a sudden become so possessive of her? And I was pretty sure that Natasha had mentioned he was at that party. There were too many common denominators.

Natasha's breathing had deepened and I knew she finally slept. My fingers were intertwined within hers. The adrenaline that had been pumping through me was finally starting to slow and I could feel my body relax and finally drift off to sleep.

⌇━━━━⌇

I was wide awake before the sun rose. I knew my parents would likely be furious with me. We'd calmed my dad down last night, and here I was only a few hours later doing exactly what we'd decided not to do last night, but I couldn't wait any longer.

Laying there in the darkness I pulled my phone out and typed a quick message.

> *We need to talk, now. The park, you remember the place.*

Surprisingly, I didn't have to wait long until I got a response.

30 mins

Carefully, I crawled over Natasha, hoping she wouldn't awaken. I found paper and a pen on her desk and wrote out a quick note letting her know I'd text her later. I didn't want the sound of her phone waking her if I sent her a text.

CHAPTER NINETEEN

~ *Troy* ~

The top of the picnic table I sat on was cold. It was still early morning. The grass and plants were still wet with moisture from the night. A few joggers were already out on their early morning run, as the city was awakening from its slumber.

The years had changed this area, but minimally. The swing set we used to play on as kids was still a fixture. There was a winding path that ran through the park we'd ridden our bikes and scooters on. A newer play set had been added near the swings. This had always been our favorite place as kids. We played here, we had birthday parties here, even as we got older, we'd still hang out here.

The last time I remembered all of us being here was Memorial Day before Talise and Caleb graduated. Both our families and the offices had claimed an entire corner of the park for a barbecue. There had even been games where the two offices had competed head to head. In the end it had been a tie, but no one cared. Everyone had enjoyed themselves and it was the last time life had felt normal.

Caleb's truck pulled up along the side of the street the bordered the park. We made eye contact as he walked toward me. Caleb had a bit of a height advantage on me and was stockier, but somehow, I still always saw him as the scrawny little kid that he used to be. It looked like he'd slept off whatever alcohol he'd consumed last night. His stride was determined, if not a bit angry.

"What's with all the urgency? You know it's a Saturday morning, right?" Caleb asked as he reached the picnic table and sat at the opposite end.

"I'm actually a little bit surprised you answered, and showed up," I stated.

"Curious, I guess, you haven't talked to me in over three years. Why now?"

"What was going on last night with Natasha? You had her pinned to the wall."

"I did not. I was just talking with her. Don't get your panties in such a bundle. She just started freaking out. I didn't do anything to her."

Anger was quickly consuming me. "Caleb, you had hold of her arm. I saw it."

"She tripped. I was just trying to make sure she didn't fall, and then she started freaking out. Is this all you wanted to talk to me about? I get it. She's with you now. Leave her alone. Is that want you wanted to say?"

"She's her own person Caleb. I won't tell her who she can talk to and who she can't. That's her decision."

"So why did you bring me all the way out here at the butt crack of dawn on a Saturday morning?"

"I wanted to talk about Talise."

"Tailse? What about Talise? That was a long time ago."

"Why did you guys break up?"

"Seriously? Come on Troy. What does it matter? It was three years ago. She's gone. Move on."

"Something happened between the two of you. I want to know what it was. I want you to tell me. I deserve that, Caleb."

"Bro, she was the one that broke it off with me. Wouldn't talk to me. She broke my heart. She was the love of my life. I'd loved her for a long time before we even started dating. I didn't do anything. It wasn't my fault. I don't understand why you want to talk about this now. She just stopped talking to me. I don't know why. We had been talking about the future. She was all I ever wanted. She crushed me when she left. And really, I thought maybe you'd talk to me. I came to you asking you for help, to find out why she wasn't talking to me anymore. But what did you do? You ghosted me. You were like a brother to me growing up and then nothing. You stopped hanging out. You stopped talking to me. I lost her too. She died under your watch. You were so busy you didn't have time for anyone. You were supposed to be there for her, for me, for both of us. I thought we were family. You turned your back on me, just like she did."

"She said things were over, that you'd had an argument. That things weren't going to work anymore. I didn't press her. I trusted her judgement. She could make her own decisions."

"You knew her. You knew me. In one moment, you just let it all go?"

"Something was off. I knew something was off with her. But before I could really talk to her, she was gone. And every time I saw you after, it brought back all that pain. But now, now I know what you did, and it was unforgivable."

"What I did? What are you talking about? I already told you. I didn't do anything. She was the one that broke it off."

"Really? You did nothing? What about raping her Caleb?" I tried to keep my voice calm and composed as I stared directly at Caleb.

"Raping her? What the fuck, are you talking about?"

"The graduation party. That night you raped her." Caleb's face started to get red splotches. Something that happened when he was a kid and would get angry. I knew I'd pushed a button with him.

"Bro, you need to stop. You have no idea what you're talking about. I never raped her. I never even slept with her! What the fuck are you talking about?"

"Really? That's not what she says."

"Are you talking to ghosts now? She's dead, how the hell is she 'talking'? Come on. Seriously what is all this about."

"You raped her. She said no. But you didn't listen, you took her anyways. You ripped her clothes that night, do you remember that?"

"You're clearly delusional. We were all drinking. We were having fun. We had just graduated. I did not rape her."

"You both were in the bathroom. She tried to stop you. You didn't stop. You took her to a bedroom and raped her."

Caleb stood up slamming his fist onto the picnic table. "I've had enough of this bullshit Troy. You don't know what the fuck you are talking about. How dare you come up with these crazy ass stories three years after she died. I can't believe you'd even think I'd do something like this! I loved her! I was heartbroken when she wouldn't take my calls, when she wouldn't talk to me."

"Because you raped her! Why the hell would she talk to you? She trusted you! I trusted you!"

"Again, I don't know what you are talking about! I never raped her. I repeat, I never even slept with her!"

"Come on Caleb, really? Then why did she write in her journal about how she was in the bedroom and you wouldn't stop and ripped her clothing?"

"Troy, seriously I don't know what you are talking about! She passed out, I carried her to one of the bedrooms and when I came back for her, she was gone. I don't know what you're trying to do here. You have no right to throw these accusations at me! I'm done, I'm out of here. I didn't do anything to her!" He turned and started walking toward his truck.

"She was pregnant, Caleb."

Caleb stopped dead in his tracks as he spun around. "What did you just say?"

"She was pregnant."

"Not possible. I told you I didn't have sex with her."

"She was pregnant. I saw the ultrasound photo."

"Oh. So, what you are saying is she cheated on me? Is that what this is all about? Are you trying to hurt me after all this time? It's your fault she isn't alive today. She used to always tell me how busy you were, how everyone always catered to you. You were the golden child. You didn't have time for her, you were too busy with everything else in your life. So, don't come here blaming me for her being messed up so badly that she decided to end her own life."

"What happened? Did she tell you she was pregnant?"

"Bro, I told you she stopped talking to me after the graduation party. But it's all making more sense now. She must have hooked up with someone else at that party and then felt so guilty about it she broke it off with me."

I was off that picnic bench before I even knew what I was doing. Rage had boiled over and the next thing I knew, both Caleb and I were on the ground.

~ *Natasha* ~

The cold woke me, I was curled up on my side. I reached for my blanket to curl up in so that I could get back asleep. I was exhausted. It had been a rough night and I felt like I could sleep for days.

Wait, where was Troy? I never felt him move. He had kept me warm, through the night, and now without him the room was chilly. Maybe he was just in the bathroom. Sitting up I realized that the bathroom door was open and it didn't look like he was still here. Why didn't he wake me?

Grabbing my phone from the nightstand, the only text was from Justine saying she wouldn't be back to the dorm until this evening. Wow, not even a text from Troy? Where did he run off to?

My eye caught the note on the desk.

> You needed your sleep. Had something I needed to take care of, couldn't wait. I'll text you later. Didn't want to wake you.

A HEALING TOUCH

What was so important that it couldn't wait? I sent him a text.

> Natasha
> *I'm up. Where are you?*
> *Are you okay?*

While I waited for him to respond, I cleaned up and got dressed. Still no response.

> Natasha
> *Okay, I'm getting a little worried. A lot happened last night. Where are you?*

> Troy
> *I'm okay, I need to talk to Caleb.*

> Natasha
> *Troy, No. Please don't. This is not a good idea right now.*

> Troy
> *I need to do this Natasha. I'll text you later.*

> Natasha
> *Troy, where are you?*

My heart was pounding. Why would he go and confront Caleb? I thought they had decided to hold off until they got more information. I waited for Troy to respond and nothing. I couldn't just sit here. Where had he gone? I quickly texted Camille to see if she had heard from Troy. I was beginning to get desperate.

Camille
I'm sorry hun. We haven't heard from Troy since you both left last night.

Natasha
I'm worried about him. He left sometime this morning. He just responded to my text and all he said was that he needed to talk to Caleb.

Camille
OMG Natasha, we need to find them!

Natasha
I asked him where he was, he never responded. Do you have any idea where they would have gone?

A HEALING TOUCH

Camille
I have no idea, ever
since Talise passed,
they really haven't
spoken. Let me make
some calls. If I find
anything out I'll let you
know.

Natasha
Okay, I'm going to get in
my car and start driving
around. I have to do
something, I can't just sit
here and wait.

Grabbing my sweatshirt, I locked the door and practically ran to my car. Where I was going, I had no idea. They could be anywhere. I called Kelsey from the car. She'd known Troy a long time. I knew it was still early. She probably wouldn't even pick up, but I had to try her. I was about to hang up, when Kelsey finally answered.

"Hey Natasha, you okay?"

She sounded groggy, I felt bad for waking her this early in the morning. "Yeah, I'm okay."

"I'm sorry you missed the awards last night. They said you got sick?"

"I'll tell you about it later. Ummm...I know you and Troy go way back. How much do you know about his and Caleb's friendship?"

"Caleb? There is no friendship. I mean I guess not anymore. When I first met Troy, I know they hung out together more. Well I guess it was actually their families that hung out together. Why? What's with all the questions?"

"Kelsey, I can't get into all that right now, it's not my place. But I need to find Troy and I know that he is meeting with Caleb. Or at least I'm going to try and find him."

"Okay, now you really have my curiosity up, what is going on?"

"I need to find Troy, I'm in my car leaving campus. Do you have any idea where they might go? Did they have a restaurant they went to, or a place they hung out? Did you ever go with them? Any ideas?"

"I don't really know. That was so long ago."

"Kelsey, please think."

"There's a 24-hour diner not far from the office, Callie's. I know we'd eat there a lot. Have you ever been there?"

"No, but I know where it is. Anywhere else?"

"Ummm...let me think."

"I know it's like a needle in a haystack, but I can't just sit here and wait for Troy to text me back."

"Wait, there was a park, we'd have office barbecues at University Park. It's kind of on your way to Callie's. Caleb's family would come too most of the times. Other than those two specific places I really don't know. They really could be anywhere Natasha, are you sure everything is okay? Now you have me worried."

"I don't know. I really don't know. I'll let you know if I find him."

"Okay. Good Luck."

"Thanks, Kelsey."

Exiting campus, I headed south on my wild goose chase. The streets were still quiet, and mostly empty this early on a Saturday morning. My mind raced through all the different scenarios. University Park wasn't far. If I remembered correctly, Justine had shown it to me when I first got to school in the fall. It stuck in my memory because there was a cute little book library on one of the corners. I'd circle the block where the park was first before trying Callie's diner.

The park was not much further. I slowed my car as I neared, searching the grassy area in the distance for any signs of Troy or Caleb when I realized that both Troy's and Caleb's cars were parked along the street. I parked behind Troy's corvette and jumped out of my car, searching the park area. I could hear them yelling at each other as I ran toward their voices. There were picnic tables not far from the street down a small embankment with a flight of stairs. Reaching the top of the stairs, I watched in horror as Troy leaped off the picnic table he'd been sitting on and tackled Caleb to the ground.

"Troy, No! Stop!" I screamed as a ran down the stairs.

By the time I reached them they were practically rolling around on the ground. Arms and fists flying as they screamed at each other. I kept screaming both of their names, but it seemed that neither heard me or even acknowledged that I was standing there. I didn't know how to make them stop and I didn't want anyone getting hurt. I knew that Troy was angry and frustrated, but this was not the way to handle it.

Before I really thought about what I was doing, I crouched down where they were on the ground and tried to grab Troy's arms and pull him away. And then there was nothing but silence and blackness.

~ *Troy* ~

Caleb was strong, but the anger and hurt that had built up in me propelled me forward. I wasn't thinking anymore and I knew this was childish and stupid, but my little sister was gone. She was never coming back. All I could think about was that Caleb was the one responsible for that.

I felt hands grabbing my arm and pulling me backward, but Caleb was directly in front of me. It had to be my mind playing tricks. Caleb swung towards me and I braced myself for the blow, but then felt nothing. But I heard the impact, and then heard a thud.

What the hell? Out of the corner of my eye, I saw her sprawled on the ground. Her dark hair tousled over her face, and without even seeing her features, I knew it was Natasha.

"Natasha!" I screamed as I untangled myself from Caleb and fell onto my knees by her side, carefully pushing her hair out of her face.

"I didn't mean it!" Caleb cried. "She came out of nowhere. I never saw her."

She was so still laying there. I didn't know if she hit her head when she fell or if it was entirely from the blow that Caleb had just landed on her face that had knocked her out. I didn't know what to do. Do I carry her to the car and take her to the hospital? Do I call 911? It was my fault that she was laying here injured. She was here because of me and my stupidity.

"Troy, this isn't my fault. She wasn't supposed to be here," Caleb yelled.

"Shut up, Caleb."

"Bro, this is all on you. You attacked me."

Leaning down, I could hear her breathing. Her cheek was already an angry red. A small cut had leaked a bit of blood down her cheek and streaked down her neck. I carefully wiped it with the edge of my sleeve. It didn't look deep and the blood looked like it had stopped. "Natasha, can you hear me?" I asked quietly.

"It wasn't my fault! I wasn't trying to hurt her. I didn't even know she was there!"

"Caleb, you hit her in the face." I screamed.

My phone kept ringing; I pulled it out of my pocket surprised that the glass wasn't cracked. Missed calls from Natasha, my mom, and Kelsey. The current ringing was Kelsey.

"Kelsey."

"Troy, what is going on? Natasha is frantic and she's out trying to find you."

"She found me."

"Okay. So, you're all good? She had me freaked out."

"No, we're not good. She's out cold. She got slugged in the face by Caleb."

"What?! What do you mean she got hit in the face? What is going on?!"

"It doesn't matter right now. I need to get help for Natasha. I'm not sure if she hit her head or if she's just knocked out from being hit."

"Call freakin 911 you idiot. Now! Where are you? I'm on my way."

"We're at University Park."

"I'll be there as soon as I can. Call 911."

Kelsey disconnected and I put my phone on speaker next to Natasha so that I had both hands free while I called 911. Caleb paced behind me. I was a bit surprised he hadn't just taken off.

Natasha groaned just as the operator was answering the 911 call. I quickly answered the operator's questions as I sat next to Natasha, carefully cradling her head in my lap. She was waking up. The 911 operator told me that the ambulance was in route and to stay put.

"Natasha, can you hear me?"

"Troy?" her bright blue eyes stared up into mine.

"Are you okay?" I asked.

"My face and head hurts. What happened?"

"You tried to get in the middle of us and you got hit."

"I didn't know what to do. I was screaming at you both but neither of you were stopping."

I could feel her trying to sit up. "Stop, just stay put. There's an ambulance coming to make sure you are okay. You got knocked unconscious."

"I'm sorry, Natasha. I didn't mean to hit you," Caleb apologized from behind me and he actually sounded sincere.

"I'll be okay."

I could hear the sirens in the distance now. It wouldn't be much longer until help would be here. Natasha's head still rested in my lap. Her right arm crossed over her chest; her fingers intertwined with mine as it rested on her left shoulder.

~ *Natasha* ~

A HEALING TOUCH

My cheek stung, and throbbed. I felt dazed, but all I really wanted to do was to get Troy out of here and away from Caleb. The sirens stopped and I assumed that meant that they were at the park.

"So, what happened here?" The paramedic's voice was deep, his dark hair was streaked with gray. He was soothing and calm, directing his gaze at Troy but was eyeing both boys.

"She got hit in the face, and she was out cold."

His partner was petite, younger, her blond hair pulled into a sleek ponytail, she kneeled next to me as she set her bag on the damp grass. "Hi, I'm Lara. What's your name?"

"Natasha. I'm fine."

"I'm sure you are, but why don't you let us make sure, okay?" Lara smiled as she checked my blood pressure and pulse. "Where do you hurt?"

"It's just my face. It stings. And I feel dumb. I shouldn't have tried to get in the middle of them."

"Yeah, boys aren't very smart sometimes. Were they fighting over you?" Lara asked as she ran her fingers across my face.

"Um, I don't think so. I found them like that."

"Okay, let's try to sit you up. Did she lose consciousness?" Lara asked over my shoulder at Troy.

"I think so, but not for long," Troy answered.

I pushed myself into a sitting position with Troy behind me and Lara the paramedic in front of me. She looked me over, checked my vitals, cleaned my forehead and placed a bandage over where the blood had trickled from a cut. After what seemed like several minutes I was allowed to stand up.

"Do you want to go to the hospital to get further checked out?" Lara asked while her partner gathered up their gear.

"No, I'm okay."

"Okay, but if you start to feel nauseous, or you start to feel worse, get yourself down to the ER. You're going to probably have a black eye. Keep some ice on it to reduce swelling. Take some Tylenol or Advil to help with the pain. And you guys, are you good? Or do we need to get the cops down here?"

"No, we're good." Both Troy and Caleb answered almost in unison.

I walked over to the picnic table and sat down as the paramedics loaded up and left the park. I looked over at both Troy and Caleb standing several feet apart from each other. They both were going to have some bruising and soreness from their tussle on the ground.

"Enough! Both of you! Just stop."

"Honestly, Natasha, I didn't mean to hit you!" Caleb once again apologizing.

"I know. I was just in the wrong place at the wrong time. But why were you guys rolling around on the ground? Troy, I thought we weren't going to do anything right now?" I held the ice pack that had been left with me tight against my burning cheek. Watching both of them stand there.

Caleb's head snapped toward me in astonishment. "What? Seriously?! What is going on with both of you? Troy brings me down here and starts accusing me of raping Talise! I never laid a hand on her! I loved her!"

"Caleb, she said you raped her," I stated quietly.

"I don't understand! You never met her. She's been gone for three years. Three years! Where is this coming from now? How would you know what she said? That doesn't even make any sense!"

"Can you guys please sit down? I'm getting a headache from looking up at you both." I watched how Caleb answered and I began to wonder if maybe he wasn't telling the truth. Or at least what he believed to be the truth. Something here wasn't quite right and I wasn't sure what it was.

Troy slid in next to me, and wrapped his arm around my waist pulling me closer to him.

"He came at me first. I wasn't doing anything. I was just defending myself." Caleb stated as he finally sat down across the picnic table glaring at Troy.

"Talise wrote it all down Caleb, so you can just stop with your lying," Troy spit out.

I could feel his anger radiating off him as I watched the two of them stare at each other across the table.

"Troy, I'm telling you, I never touched her! I wouldn't have done that to her!"

"She said you were drunk, but even drunk that's no excuse. How could you?"

"Come on, seriously. You know me, or at least I thought you did. Why would you think I could do that to her. I'm telling you I didn't touch her! She disappeared that night. The next morning when I tried to call her and talk to her she wouldn't talk to me. I don't know what happened! She shattered my world, Troy! I still miss her every single day!"

"Why would she lie Caleb? Especially about that? And she didn't tell anyone, she just wrote it in her journal."

"I don't know. I don't even know why you're accusing me now of all this? What happened?"

I watched the expressions flicker across Caleb's face as he and Troy threw accusations at each other. Caleb almost looked defeated, crushed, and even confused. Not what I expected to see.

"Caleb, we found missing pages from Talise's journal last night. She had ripped them out and had them hidden away. We discovered them when we were sorting through some of her things. She wrote that the night of the graduation party, when you guys were in the bathroom, things started to get heated between you both. That she told you to slow down and to stop. Then she woke up in a bedroom and you were holding her down and raped her."

"What?! I didn't do that! I'm telling you I never touched her! She was still passed out when I left the bedroom. And when I returned, she was gone. The next day when I tried to talk to her, she wouldn't talk to me! I wouldn't have done that to her! I need to see what she wrote. Because I'll tear apart the mother fucker that touched her! And Troy, seriously I can't believe that you'd actually believe I'd do something like that. Bro, we grew up together. I'd never hurt her like that!"

"You've not been the same since that night, Caleb! Even recently, the couple of times I've seen you around Natasha, you've been angry, and possessive. I wouldn't have expected that from you either!"

"Because, you destroyed everything, Troy! All the times our families were together and then it was just over. Not only did I lose Talise, but I lost a brother! My parents were planning our futures. For three years that's all I've heard from my parents! How I must have messed things up with Talise. And then Natasha comes into the picture and you snap her up too."

"But you didn't ever seem interested in me, Caleb. I liked you; I really did. I'd had a crush on you almost all year. But it was like you only started to talk to me outside of class after you found out I was interviewing at Troy's family office."

Silence settled over the picnic table, everyone seemed to be in their own thoughts, but I was beginning to believe Caleb. Could there be some truth in what he said? Talise, by her own admission said she'd been drinking, and that she'd passed out. What if it wasn't Caleb in the room, but someone else? What if all of this had been a complete misunderstanding?

A car door shut in the distance and I could hear my name being called. Kelsey. How'd she get here? I looked over Caleb's shoulder and could see her practically running down the hill toward us.

"Oh my God! Natasha! Your face!" Kelsey's horrified statement made me feel even more self-conscious about how bad I must really look now.

"I'm fine, Kelsey. How'd you know we were here?" I stood up to accept the hug she offered.

"Troy finally answered his phone and said you'd been knocked out. What the hell is going on here?" Kelsey stood firm, pointing at both Troy and Caleb. "You both look like you've gone a few rounds. Why are you fighting? You've barely spoken but a few words to each other in over three years. Is this over Natasha?"

"Kelsey, really, I'm fine. But they need to sort some things out. It's not about me. It's about Talise."

"Talise?" Kelsey questioned. "What about Talise?"

"Honestly, Kelsey, it's a long story and we don't have the whole thing put together yet. How about I call you later okay?"

Kelsey turned to me and then looked back between both Troy and Caleb. "Are you sure you're okay?"

"Yes, please. It's okay. Thank you for checking on me though." I leaned over and gave her a big hug and whispered into her ear. "It's a family thing they need to work out."

"Okay. But you better call me later," Kelsey whispered back.

"I promise."

I sat back down next to Troy. The tension between the two of them was stifling. It was like I wasn't even there. They were both locked onto each other. I wasn't sure where to go from here. So many things didn't make sense.

"I need to see those pages, Troy. I don't understand what happened." Caleb's voice was low, the anger had vanished and there was nothing left but pain.

"Troy, maybe we should let him." My hand rested on his leg, offering whatever encouragement I could. "Maybe we've missed something. Maybe Talise missed something. Think about it. She even said she'd blacked out. The room was dark. She never said Caleb said anything to her, she just assumed it was him since he was the last person she *did* remember being with. It is possible that someone else got into that room after Caleb left."

Troy shifted his stare from Caleb to me. Silence. I could tell he was wrestling with a decision. His jaw twitched. I knew he was struggling with everything that had just landed in his lap.

"Okay." His voice was filled with resignation.

"Okay." I repeated. I looked over at Caleb. "If you are telling the truth, reading those pages isn't going to be easy."

"Wondering for the last three years what the hell happened hasn't been easy either," Caleb responded.

"Let's get this over with. Meet us at the house. I'll show you the pages. But I swear, if you're lying, and you did do what she said in those pages, I'll find a way to make you pay for what you did to her." Troy's voice was laced with tension.

"I didn't hurt her, Troy. I wish you would believe that. I'll follow you over there."

CHAPTER TWENTY

~ *Troy* ~

𝒞*aleb's* words kept running through my head as we drove toward my house. Natasha sat in the passenger seat, still holding the ice pack against the left side of her face. I had suggested that she leave her car there at the park and that we'd come back for it later.

I still couldn't believe she'd been collateral damage. I knew I'd probably have a few bruises and some aches and pains after the adrenaline finally wore out of me. Caleb had gotten in a few good hits. I'd never lost my temper like that before. I didn't want Natasha to think that fighting like that was a common thing for me.

But what if what Caleb said was true? What if Talise got it wrong? She'd never talked to anyone, so there wasn't anyone to ask her questions, or to be sure what she saw, was really what she saw.

What got to me the most was the pain in Caleb's eyes as he'd accused me of even thinking he could do something like that to Talise. Deep down when I really started thinking about it, what he said rang true. I never had expected anything like that from Caleb. Did I think he was a bit spoiled? Absolutely. But he was right; we had been like brothers, and I really didn't reach out to him after Talise had said they were over. I was so focused on my school and work and having that thrown back in my face only made my guilt over everything intensify.

I was so outraged by how hurt Talise had been, how she'd not told a soul about what had happened to her. Maybe I had been over reacting to everything and immediately threw blame at Caleb because that was the easiest. Talise had written the words. I had only taken them at face value without looking beyond what she had said. Her words fueled my anger and frustration that had already been there simmering under the surface.

It was Natasha's quiet summary that started the questions. The first crack in the story. Caleb was correct, I did owe him a chance to explain his side. I had abandoned him. He was completely right, and I owed it to him to at least hear him out.

Glancing in my rear-view mirror confirmed that Caleb was still behind us as we drove through town that was just starting to awaken from its slumber.

"How do you think your parents are going to react to Caleb being in the house?" Natasha asked.

"Maybe they'll still be sleeping and won't know?" I replied with a slight smile.

"Um. I doubt that. I kind of already texted Camille when I was looking for you. So I know she's up, and she's probably worried about you."

"Great, she'll probably be even more upset when she sees that you took a hit. She's never going to let me live that one down."

~ *Caleb* ~

Following Troy's car through the streets, I was still stunned. Talise was raped? I couldn't believe it. It didn't make any sense. And how could Troy really believe I'd do that to Talise? I wasn't sure which was worse, that Talise had apparently written in a journal that she'd been raped. Or that whatever she'd written and Troy actually believed I would have done that.

I'd relived that night at the party over and over in my head trying to piece together what had happened. I'd never been able to make sense out of why after all those years together that Talise had completely shut me out.

When the call came that she'd died and it looked like suicide I was in complete shock. Talise wasn't that person! Not the Talise I knew. And pregnant? What the hell was Troy talking about? There was no way she was pregnant. We'd never had sex. I'd wanted to, many, many times, but the timing had never been right. We'd get interrupted or something came up, it just hadn't happened.

I had thought maybe that night at the graduation party maybe that night might be the night. But she had drank a little too much and then she'd passed out. I made sure she was safe and out of the way. I hadn't even been gone that long. I literally had gone downstairs to find Talise's friends and let them know I was going to call an Uber and take her home. By the time I'd gotten back upstairs where I'd left her, she was gone. It had freaked me out.

I'd been texting and calling her, trying to figure out where she'd gone. I had been worried about her. I'd gone back downstairs searching through everyone downstairs and outside, but no one had seen her. I'd gone from drunk to sober in a heartbeat.

I worried all night. The following morning I'd finally shown up at her house looking for her. Her mom had answered the door and said she was home, but asleep. I'd finally been able to calm down enough knowing she was home. I thought I'd talk to her after I'd gotten some sleep. But later in the day she was still not returning my calls. And then the next thing I know she's telling me it's all over. I couldn't believe it. I had no idea what had happened. What had gone wrong? Why was she shutting me out? And it wasn't just me. It was everyone that she'd shut down.

By the end of the summer, I was at my wits end. I'd tried so hard to get her to talk to me, but she wouldn't. Then she was gone and I was left with my grief and my unanswered questions. I thought we'd be together forever. We'd practically grown up together. She'd been a part of my life for as long as I could remember.

One minute we were celebrating graduation and moving on to the next phase of our lives. The next minute, everything I'd hoped for was shattered into a million pieces. I didn't know if I'd ever get over her.

Three years later and she still invaded my thoughts. Even as I tried to push them away. I'd dated casually over the years, but nothing that was serious. I just couldn't take that next step. The girls had been a revolving door. Once I started to feel like they were getting too connected, I'd break it off.

The first time I'd seen Natasha in the studio I'd sensed something different about her. In three years, she was the first girl that I felt a pull that I'd had with Talise. There was something about her. I'd watch her from afar, and sat in several of her studio presentations, but mostly kept my distance. Until the final quarter last year. I'd stopped by her desk more frequently, offered her more help. Any reason at all to talk to her, but I could never really pull the trigger and ask her out. I don't know what always stopped me. I usually had no problem asking girls out, but not Natasha.

Then at the very end of school, she showed up at a party. I'd never seen her come to any of the parties on campus during the entire year, but there she was. I remembered even what she was wearing. When I saw her, I thought okay, this is easy, just ask her to dance. Keep it casual. When she practically fell into my arms I felt a shock race through me, none that I had felt since Talise.

But something was wrong with her that night. She practically fell to the floor, and it was all I could do to pull her upright and ended up carrying her outside to get some fresh air. Her words had been slurred and it was hard to understand what she was saying. I asked her if I could take her back to her dorm. At first, she said yes, but then she refused. She wasn't leaving her friend alone and that she'd be fine. She was just going to wait right there on the steps for her friend.

I knew something was wrong. I sat with her for a while. She seemed to be feeling better with the fresh air and then the guys I was with were leaving and dragged me along. I asked her one last time if she needed a ride, but she refused. She said she was feeling better, that she just needed to sit a bit longer in the fresh cool air. I left, but I told her if she needed me all she'd need to do was text me and I'd be there. She never texted.

Then I found out she was interviewing with DeLuca Architects, and I was angry. I was still hurt and angry at Troy. When Talise died, I lost not only her, but I'd lost part of my extended family too. I wanted her to come work with us. I don't know why I hadn't thought about it earlier in the year, but it was like a trigger. As soon as I knew she was interviewing somewhere else, I was jealous. I don't even know why I was so jealous, I just was.

Running into her with Troy the couple of times that I had during the summer just added to the resentment. The anger was starting to boil over. Seeing her at the awards ceremony had been rough. She'd looked so beautiful. I tried to stay away. I knew I'd had a few too many drinks. My parents had given me that look. One I'd seen way too many times over the last few years. That disappointed look that crushed my soul. I knew I'd never be good enough for them. They were always comparing me to Troy. I knew I would never live up to their expectations.

I'd seen Natasha get up and leave the main reception hall before the program. I had followed her into the restroom hallway. I hadn't meant to startle her, and I really did think she was going to fall. But then she freaked out on me, I could see the fear in her eyes. She was afraid of me. It cut me to the core. Why would she be afraid of me? I'd never done anything to her. And then Troy came running in the middle of it just making things worse.

Watching him pull her away from me like I was some sort of monster was the end. I was done for the night. I didn't care who won what award anymore. I didn't care if my parents were going to be pissed at me for leaving. I was out of there. I almost drove myself home, but I knew deep down that driving in my condition would not have made anything better only worse. So, I waited out front for an Uber to pick me up. I couldn't get out of there fast enough.

When the text from Troy came through this morning, I had already sobered up and was on my way home from picking up my truck from the event center where I'd left it. I had no idea what he wanted to talk about, but I didn't really care. I was still angry. What more could he say to me anyway?

I had not been expecting the accusations about Talise, though. I was still in complete disbelief. I had to read these so-called journal pages that Troy was talking about. Until I saw them myself there was no way I could just accept what he was telling me.

~ *Troy* ~

Sadie was waiting for us in the entryway. Her tail thumping rapidly on the hard wood floor. Coffee brewing in the kitchen answered my question regarding my parents being up already. I wasn't sure how they were going to react to Caleb being here. Especially after what we'd all read last night in Talise's journal pages. Honestly, I wasn't even sure how I felt about Caleb being here.

Natasha leaned down to pet Sadie and she let out a soft whine in greeting. Then she noticed Caleb behind me and circled him nudging his hand. Even though it had been years since Caleb had stepped foot in the house, Sadie had not forgotten him.

My dad was sitting at the island bar with a mug in his hand and a half-eaten bagel in front of him. My mom was grabbing something from the fridge and stopped to give me the look that said she wasn't happy with me.

"Troy, are you okay? Natasha was looking for you this morning. She said you were out meeting with Caleb. I thought we talked about that last night."

"Actually, she's here with me, and so is Caleb."

My dad immediately sat his mug on the counter and stood up. "What?"

The door to the fridge shut a little harder than normal and I knew that neither of my parents were very pleased about this turn of events.

Natasha's hand slid into mine as I felt her lean up against my side.

"I think we're missing something. I know what we all thought last night but please, I think Caleb has a right to see the pages that Talise wrote. He swears that he never touched her." Natasha explained.

Both of my parents tensed as Caleb moved further into the kitchen. Sadie was next to him licking his hand and wagging her tail.

"I loved Talise. I'd never hurt her. I didn't touch her and I didn't do what she said. You both were like another set of parents to me. Troy, a brother. How could you even think I'd do that? I need to see what she wrote because I don't understand what happened."

"Well, something happened to her, Caleb, because after the night of the graduation party she was never the same. She was there with you. Her words were pretty specific, and she's gone now so it's pretty easy for you to discredit or try to deny anything happened because she's not here to defend herself."

"I get it, but I lost her too. Our families spent so much time together. You know me. You've known me all my life. I'm telling the truth. I never touched her, and if I ever find out who did hurt her God help them. Please. I need to see these pages that were found."

"Troy, go ahead," my mom whispered as she pointed toward Talise's room.

~ *Caleb* ~

Walking into Talise's room was like stepping back in time. Three years to be exact. I could still feel her presence in the room. Her laughter, her teasing, the endless hours spent hanging out in this room. I couldn't believe everything was still in the same place that I remembered. Nothing had changed.

Troy walked over to Talise's desk and picked up several sheets of paper that had been laying there folded up and handed them to me. Talise's familiar handwriting made my breath catch. She had always been leaving me notes here and there that were funny, mostly nonsense, but it had always made me smile. I'd missed her humor and laugher the most. She'd always had a way to make you feel better when everything else seemed to be going wrong.

I sat down on her bench at the foot of the bed, the pages that I held in my hands holding her most intimate secrets. On one hand, based on what Troy and Natasha had told me, I almost feared to read her words, but I had to know. I had to know why she'd turned so cold toward me and wouldn't talk to me.

June fifteenth, the night after the graduation party. As I read through each word, and re-read each word, I was numb. Who the hell had done this to her? How could she have thought it was me? How did she get home?

I moved to the next page, my hands trembling with anger. Oh my God, she was pregnant? So many things were starting to fall into place now. No wonder she was so withdrawn, but I still didn't understand how could she think it had been me?

Each page was harder to read than the next page. How could this have happened? Why? Why didn't she reach out to anyone? Her friends, or her family would have helped. I would have helped her if she'd just talked to me. It was like losing her all over again, but almost worse. Feeling her despair, the hopelessness in her words shattered me.

Even at the end, so many more questions than answers. What happened with the pills? Her last entry sounded like she was finally starting to work things out. My heart was in a million pieces. Not only had I lost her, but the last months she was alive, she hated me. Not just a little bit, but despised me, thinking of me as a monster. She honestly thought I'd raped her. I'd never be able to mend things, to make things better. I was bitter, angry, and trying to keep back the tears I could feel threatening to escape.

Across the room, I could feel Natasha and Troy watching me. Natasha sat in the chair in front of Talise's desk with Troy behind her. His hands rested on her shoulders. I noticed both Camille and Thomas standing in the doorway also watching me.

"I didn't do this! I swear! I can't believe she really thought it was me!" my voice choked and the tears that I had been trying so hard to keep back started falling.

"She died hating me, and I never touched her. I would never, never have hurt her like that!"

The journal pages were like fire in my hands, burning me, burning my soul. Three years of anger, hurt, and resentment that had built up inside of me was pounding to get out.

But now, all I wanted to do was to hunt down who had hurt her. There had been so many people at that party. Hundreds in our graduating class, plus all the other kids that hadn't even been in our class that had been there. Besides the fact that over three years had gone by, the chances of finding the person responsible was practically an impossibility. It felt hopeless, depressing , soul crushing and I wasn't sure what I could do.

CHAPTER TWENTY-ONE

~ Natasha ~

Finals were a week away. I had been working long hours on my studio project. Troy kept me company most nights, bringing me coffee and snacks. Offering input on my design and how I was going to present it. Having him by my side made the hours fly by.

In the weeks since Talise's journal pages had been found, there seemed to be a peace that had settled on Troy and his family as well as Caleb and his family. The flashes of anger and hostility that I'd seen during the summer from Caleb were gone and it was nice to see both him and Troy getting along. They'd text and had even hung out a couple of times. I hoped that eventually they'd find reconciliation and be able to mend some of the wounds from the past few years.

Caleb seemed to be the one taking it the hardest. He now had some answers, but he was devastated knowing the details of what Talise had been going through those last few months of her life. But life is like that sometimes and you have to find your way forward. I really hoped he'd be able to do that. The chances that they'd ever know who had really hurt Talise were all but impossible at this point.

The studio was still scattered with students, but it was thinning out every hour that passed. Troy was finishing a project at work and promised to come by as soon as he was done. I wasn't sure how much longer I'd even be able to make it. The lack of sleep during the past week as starting to catch up with me.

Closing my laptop, I figured I needed to get up and stretch my legs and a quick trip to the bathroom. If I didn't hear from Troy soon, I'd likely pack it up and head back to the dorm for a nap. I had two days left before I'd have to present my project and while I was close, there was still a lot of the little details I needed to finish.

Walking around the studio I took the long way back to my table from the bathroom. Stopping here and there to see what everyone was working on. There were several classmates huddled around one of the desks asking questions. I knew the guy was in his fifth, and last year. He had come up with a pretty crazy design and it had drawn a lot of attention over the past week.

Leaning in, I was curious to see what everyone was so worked up over. He had an animation running on his screen and I watched in awe at how detailed it was. Shaking my head in amazement, I backed up, trying to slide out of the growing crowd, but managed to step on someone's foot.

"I'm so sorry!" I apologized quickly.

"No harm done," the guy mumbled and then was gone.

Huh, that was weird. He looked familiar but I couldn't place him. He rushed away and disappeared around the corner. Pushing it aside I hurried back to my table, feeling more awake and hopefully had enough energy left to work a bit longer. Grabbing my phone from my back pocket, as I sat down in my chair, I sent a text to Troy.

> *Natasha*
> *Hey there! How's it coming?*

> *Troy*
> *Good. I'm almost done then I'll come by.*

> *Natasha*
> *Okay. I'll see you soon. Text me when you're headed this way.*

> *Troy*
> *Will do.*

Setting my phone aside, I opened my laptop and logged back into my computer. Smiling, I reached for my new water bottle that Troy had given me the previous week. DeLuca Architects was printed vertically on one side while my name was printed horizontally across the lower bottom. Even after all day, there was still ice in it, the water still super cold. It was my new favorite water bottle. Knowing I'd dallied long enough I tried to focus on creating a list of things that I still needed to finish.

Completing my list, I started in on designing the template for my presentation boards. I'd blocked out the first one deciding which images I was going to use. I was trying to work on the next one but couldn't focus. I was suddenly feeling overheated and queasy.

I pulled my zip up sweatshirt off and tossed it on the back of my chair, but the feeling was getting worse. I realized then I'd not eaten since this morning. Ugh, totally my fault. I probably needed to get something in my stomach. I reached down for my bag that I usually kept some sort of snack in. Rummaging through it, I realized it was empty. I'd already gone through my stash of food.

Frustrated, I decided maybe this was a sign that I needed to stop for the night and take a break. Packing up my laptop and grabbing my bag and sweatshirt, I left the studio and started walking toward the dorm.

The cold air felt good on my heated body. The nausea I'd felt in the studio wasn't as bad outside. Halfway to the dorm, I started feeling dizzy again. I was trying to focus on the building ahead. Campus was mostly empty with scattered light poles lighting up the walkways as shadows danced in front of me. My vision started to blur and I felt almost weightless as strong arms surrounded me and I could hear my name whispered behind me.

I felt heavy. My throat dry. My head was throbbing. Great, just what I needed was a migraine. I didn't have time for a migraine. Pushing back the covers, I rolled over to call out to Justine when I realized I was not in my dorm room. *What the hell?* Okay, I'm having a nightmare. I need to wake up. Panic was starting to overcome me as I slowly began to recognize the room I was in. Wake up! *Wake up!* I kept telling myself.

A HEALING TOUCH

"Oh, good. I see you're awake," the deep voice said from the shadows in the corner of the room.

Oh my God, I'm not asleep, but I'm living my nightmare. The voice sounded familiar as I tried to make out the features and figure in the shadows. Who was in the room with me? He seemed tall, but hard to tell for sure since he was sitting. His hair was light in color. I thought I recognized him, but I couldn't put my fingers on where I'd seen him before. He almost looked like Caleb. No, it couldn't be. I tried to focus harder, but everything was still a little fuzzy and I knew my mind had to be playing tricks on me.

"Where am I?" my voice was scratchy, almost sore.

"You collapsed on the sidewalk. There wasn't anyone around, so I brought you back to my place."

"Oh. Well, thank you. I'll call my boyfriend and he'll come get me and I'll get out of your hair."

Sitting up, I looked closer at the figure in the corner and realized it wasn't Caleb, but it sure resembled him, at least in the shadows like he was currently in. Maybe it was just a coincidence that this was the room I'd woken up in so many months earlier. I didn't know if whoever had raped me was the occupant of the room, or merely just used the room, but I didn't want to find out. And then the thought hit me. Why didn't we look at who lived in this house as possible suspects?

My mind raced back over that night and the few memories that I had. Stopping myself, I needed to think about that later. Right now, I needed to focus on getting out of here. My skin was crawling and I couldn't stand to be in this room for one more second. Where was my bag? I scanned the room looking over the edge of the bed. It wasn't there. I reached for my back pocket for my phone but it was missing too.

~ *Troy* ~

I was starting to get worried. I'd been texting Natasha and getting no response. She knew I'd be finishing soon. Justine wasn't in their dorm room and hadn't heard from her recently so she wasn't any help. I had a very bad feeling in the pit of my stomach that something wasn't right. I'd even texted Caleb, knowing that he was often in the studio space with Natasha, but he hadn't seen her recently either.

Trying to calm down, I told myself that I was overreacting. She was probably in her dorm room and had fallen asleep. I knew she hadn't been sleeping much. Parking as close to her dorm as possible. I walked quickly through the darkened parking lot, to one of the side entries of the dorm, that was closest to her room.

You could tell it was almost finals. Students were up studying in nooks and crannies everywhere. I reached Natasha and Justine's room and knocked.

Nothing.

I knocked a little harder. "Natasha? Are you in there?"

Nothing. She was probably sleeping soundly and couldn't hear me. I wasn't going to start pounding on the door like a maniac. I turned the door hoping maybe it would be unlocked, but no such luck. Not that I really expected it to be unlocked. I knew both of the girls were diligent about making sure the door was locked.

Maybe her phone died and she was still in the studio. I turned and started walking briskly down the hallway practically running into Justine as I turned the corner.

"Woah! Where's the fire?" Justine asked.

"Sorry. I'm still looking for Natasha. I still haven't heard from her. She knew I was headed over here. I thought maybe she got tired and came back to her room and fell asleep.

"Well, let's go check. I'm sure that's where she is. She's not been sleeping much. I don't know how she keeps going."

Following Justine back down the hall I was calming down. I was sure we'd find her asleep. Justine was right she was probably exhausted. If that was the case, I'd just let her sleep and would catch up with her tomorrow.

Justine pulled her keys out and unlocked the door, pushing it open as quiet as she could in case Natasha was indeed asleep. I practically ran into her again as she stopped just inside the doorway. The light flipped on, as I looked inside, the room was empty.

<u>CHAPTER</u> TWENTY-TWO

~ *Troy* ~

She's not here. Don't panic. She's probably in the studio. I kept telling myself. As much as I wanted to tell myself that everything was fine, something deep down inside was telling me it wasn't.

"Troy, stop it. I see that look on your face. Come on, it's almost finals. She's probably still in the studio."

Justine spoke the words that I had just been thinking to myself.

"I know. You're probably right. I'll walk over there and see if I can find her."

"I'm done studying for the night. I'll come with you. Actually, wait. I know how to find her. I almost forgot."

"Forgot what?" I asked.

"After what happened at the end of the school year at that party, we connected our phones to share our location. I was so freaked out when I couldn't find her that night. We thought it would be safer for both of us to be able to track our locations in the future."

"Oh, I didn't even think about that. Well, where is she?" I asked.

Justine pulled her phone out of her pocket and waited. I fully expected her to say she was at the studio when I saw her zooming in on her screen and her face went white as she looked up at me.

"What?! Where is she?"

"She's at the house where that party was last year." Justine's voice was almost a whisper.

"Where is it?"

Justine handed her phone over and I located the blinking dot on the map.

"I'm going over there."

"Troy, you can't just go barging into someone's house. They can have you arrested for that."

"Well, I'm not just sitting here. Whose house is it?" I asked.

"I'm not sure exactly. I think several people rent rooms. I can't remember even who threw the party that night. Wait, maybe Caleb knows. He was there that night too."

> Troy
> Hey, one more question. Do you remember a party at the end of the school year? Justine was there and so was Natasha. Justine said you were there too.

> Caleb
> Yeah. Why?

> Troy
> Do you know who lives in that house?

Caleb
Umm, yeah, I think one of the guys that lives in the house is in the planning department.

Troy
Do you know him?

Caleb
Not really, we were in a class together last year, but that was about it. Why?

Troy
Are you still in the studio?

Caleb
About to leave, but yes.

Troy
Natasha isn't answering her phone. I'm in her dorm room with her roommate. She tracked Natasha's phone to that house where the party was last year.

Caleb

A HEALING TOUCH

Why would she or her
phone be there now?

> *Troy*
> *I have no idea, but*
> *something isn't right.*

Caleb
What do you need
from me?

> *Troy*
> *Can you meet me in the*
> *dorm parking lot and*
> *come with me to see if*
> *she's there?*

Caleb
I'll be right there.

"Well, what did he say?" Justine asked.

"He thinks one of the guys who lives there is in the planning department. He's coming over from the studio now and will go with me to the house. Hopefully, that guy is home and will let us in."

"I'm going with you."

"You don't need to come. Caleb and I can handle it."

"Hell no. She's my friend too, and I know what happened in that house. I'm coming with you."

"Okay, let's go. We're meeting Caleb in the parking lot. Wait, we can't take my car it won't fit everyone."

"We'll take mine. Come on."

Justine was a fast walker and we were standing by her car waiting for Caleb to walk over from the studio building. At this rate we probably could have just picked him up over there. I'd texted him our location and he said he was almost there and had found something he needed to show us. I wasn't sure I liked the sound of that and was now even more anxious as we waited for him to arrive.

"There he is," Justine pointed across the parking lot and waved him over.

Caleb held a water bottle in his hand. One I recognized immediately because it was the one I'd given Natasha just last week.

"Where did you find that?" I asked my voice tight.

"It was in the grass next to the sidewalk that leads from the studio to the dorm." Caleb said as he handed it to me.

"Something is very wrong," I stated as I took the bottle from him.

"Troy, she might have dropped it and never realized it. You know how much stuff she's been lugging back and forth lately." Justine tried to rationalize.

"I know, but something about this all doesn't feel right."

"Well, are we going or what?" Caleb asked.

~ *Natasha* ~

Swinging my feet off the edge of the bed, I stood up, but a wave of dizziness overcame me. I thought I was going to collapse again. I leaned my hand out to the edge of the bed to steady myself and felt an arm around my waist. I hadn't even heard the figure in the corner get up, but now, I realized he was right next to me. Touching me, as my body began to shake.

"Easy, you already fell once. You don't want to hurt yourself. You should probably lay back down."

I tried to focus on the voice. There was something vaguely familiar about him, but I couldn't put my fingers on it. Memories were dancing beyond my grasp, taunting me, teasing me.

"I'm really okay. I just need to find my phone and my bag. You can let go of me. I'm okay. I got up a little fast is all. I'm fine. Please, where is my stuff?" I asked.

"It's perfectly safe. I left it downstairs."

"Okay, well, let's go get it and I'll get a ride home. Thank you again for looking after me. I don't even know your name."

"It's Gage."

"Hi Gage, it's nice to meet you. I'm Natasha."

"I know."

"Uh, okay…" I paused. I was already creeped out, but now I was really starting to panic. Who was this guy? In the shadows I'd thought he sort of resembled Caleb, but not as much now seeing him in the light. "How do you know who I am?" I asked.

"I know a lot about you. I've seen you quite a bit in the studio building."

"Oh. Are you in the architecture program?" I asked. Maybe the nagging familiarity of him was only because I'd seen him around the studios and nothing more than that.

"Not the architecture program but part of the College of Design. More specifically the planning department."

I started to drop my guard a bit. Maybe this was all a crazy coincidence. But honestly, I didn't want to stay here in this room, in this house, for one second longer. Gage had dropped his arm from my waist but he still stood directly in front of me. His fingers lightly traced the side of my face and carefully tucked a stray piece of my hair behind my ear. The hair on the back of my neck stood on end.

"Wait, you were in the studio tonight. I stepped on your foot." He looked shocked, and I was pretty sure he was the one that had rushed off tonight. "Can I get my things now?" I asked, my voice starting to shake. There was definitely something not right here.

Trying to move to the side, Gage moved in front of me, blocking my exit. My heart was pounding in my chest. I wanted to scream, but didn't know if there was anyone else in the house. The neighborhood was quiet. The house was quiet. It had been late when I was in the studio and I had no idea what time it was now. I knew I needed to stay calm because panicking right now was not going to help me.

"You need to rest," Gage stated, his hand now on my shoulder guiding me back to the bed.

"No, really, I'm good. Thank you for your concern though, but I really need to get back to my dorm. My roommate will be worried about me."

"I'm sure she won't think much of it. She'll probably assume you're with your boyfriend. It's Troy, isn't it?"

Realization was hitting me very quickly that I likely had a stalker. But even more scary were the notes I'd received, and what had happened to me in this very room several months ago. I knew it had to have come from someone who had close proximity to me. Now I wondered if I had my answer on where they had come from.

Looking beyond Gage's shoulder, I was estimating how quickly could I make it to the door. But with him being right next to me, I wasn't sure I'd even have a chance. He'd probably grab me before I'd even get a step away from the bed. *Think, Natasha, think!*

"You're right. I really am not feeling very good. Maybe I should lie down for a minute. Maybe you could get me something to drink from downstairs?"

"Lay down, and I'll go get you some water."

I laid down on the bed. Hoping that with him leaving the room I'd have a chance to run. Gage said my things were downstairs. I'd try to find them if I could, but I was more concerned with getting out of this room. I was pretty sure I'd kicked my shoes under the bed when I got up. I knew I was in my socks and there had been something on the floor by the bed. If they weren't there then I'd run in my socks.

Gage backed away from the bed as I laid down. His eyes never leaving me as he moved toward the door. My heart was racing. I had to get out of here. He eventually left the room closing the door behind him. I waited a minute before I jumped out of the bed looking down for my shoes. One was visible and I grabbed it while searching for the other one that was just out of my grasp under the bed. Deciding I'd give it one last try before abandoning it, I was finally able to grab a shoelace and pull it toward me.

Sliding my feet into my shoes, I didn't even bother with tying the laces. I practically ran to the door, but trying to be as light on my feet as possible. I had no idea if the floor boards would creak and give me away. I reached for the door and turned it only to find it had somehow been locked from the outside.

Frustrated, I turned to the nearby window wondering if I could escape that way. I knew I was on the second floor but not sure if there might be a low roof I could climb down onto. I peered through the horizontal blinds and wanted to cry. It was straight down and there wasn't anything near to help get me down. There was no way I was getting out through the window.

The door knob started to move, and I froze. Do I bolt back for the bed? Do I try to hide and then make a run for it when he moved away from the door? I ran out of time when the door swung open and I was caught standing there.

Gage was frowning as he looked me over and shut the door behind him. "Well, looks like you're feeling better. I thought you'd be a little more thankful that I'd rescued you."

"I am, but I'm feeling better now. I do thank you, but I'd like to leave now. Please."

"Why? You're finally back where you belong. You were chosen."

"Chosen? What are you talking about?" I whispered, the alarm inside of me growing by the minute.

"You were the chosen one. But you also ended up being even more special. Because you were pure. I did not expect that," Gage explained.

I stood there in utter disbelief. My mind racing back to that horrible night, so many months ago. This was my worst nightmare coming true, right in front of me.

"What?" the question barely audible as it slipped from my lips.

"The water bottles, the night of the party. One was special, for a special person. It was always random, but that night, you chose it. I was watching to see who would pick it up. You were the lucky one. It was a special treat. When I saw you leave and sit outside, I thought everything was ruined. But then, then my luck turned and you sat there by yourself. Like you were waiting for me to come to you. It was meant to be. Don't you see? It was fate that brought us together and together we were something special that doesn't always come along. I was your first, and no matter what, I will always be your first," Gage smiled as he explained.

Now I was even more frightened. Not knowing quite what I was dealing with, but clearly, he was not firing on all cylinders. I was angry, and scared, but also spitting mad. How dare he! How dare assault me like that and then think we were meant to be? He was delusional if he thought there was any chance that I was his fate, or destiny, or whatever crap he'd just spewed at me.

"Move. Move now. I'm leaving." I said, firmer now. He might be taller and stronger than me but I was getting the hell out of here.

Downstairs, I could hear someone start pounding on the front door, the doorbell ringing over and over.

"You better go answer that. It sounds urgent." I stated, looking for my chance to escape this hell I'd found myself in.

"They will go away. Tending to you is more important." Gage said, as he stepped closer to me.

Backing up, I bumped into the dresser. I was looking for something I could use to protect myself. I faintly recalled seeing a lamp or something sitting on top of the dresser. My hand was behind my back feeling for it. With my luck it was probably on the other side of the dresser out of my reach. Then I felt it, just beyond my grasp. I was unable to get a grip on it though as it fell and crashed to the floor.

"Well, that wasn't very nice. You broke it." Gage said as he stepped closer to me.

"I'm really sorry I didn't mean to." I had no intention of making him angry. That would only make things worse. I was sure.

Gage was almost directly in front of me. I had slid away from the dresser moving toward the bed, but angling for the door. I didn't see that he'd locked the door. If I could reach it first, I might be able to get out of here. He took one more step toward me and I took my chance. I kicked upward as hard as I could. Aiming directly for between his legs, hoping my aim was true. When he howled in pain and fell to his knees, I ran.

I flung the door open and didn't look back. I ran down the hall and toward the stairs, grabbing the handrail I took the stairs as fast as I could. I didn't want to take a tumble down them either. The front door was in my sights.

Out of the corner of my eye, the bright turquoise of my laptop bag caught my attention. It was on the floor, almost under a side table. It was so dark down here I almost didn't see it. I hadn't looked behind me to see if Gage was there, but by the time I reached the bottom of the stair I spared a quick second to glance back up the stairs. To my relief, it was empty. I veered slightly to the right and swooped down to grab my laptop bag. My luck was holding, as my purse was sitting under it. Grabbing it as well, I ran to the front door flinging it open.

CHAPTER TWENTY-THREE

~ *Troy* ~

Justine was on a mission as she sped through the streets, but I didn't care. All I knew was we needed to get to that house and Natasha. I sure hoped it wasn't going to be a fluke like her phone being stolen. But it all didn't make sense. Why was she at this random house? Especially one where something so traumatic had happened to her. The only explanation was she was not there by choice and that made my adrenaline skyrocket.

The atmosphere in the car was rifled with tension. The only sound was the radio in the background. Thankfully, it was a quick drive and Justine parked her car along the curb. The three doors flying open and slamming shut almost simultaneously. The three of us ran up the sidewalk and the couple of steps to the covered porch of the house that Justine's tracking had led us to. Reaching the door first, I started pounding on it and ringing the doorbell.

"What are we going to do if no one opens the door?" Justine asked.

"Someone's got to be here. I think there are several roommates that rent rooms." Caleb replied.

"Okay, well, what's our backup plan if no one comes to the door?" I asked.

"Call the police?" Justine answered.

"And say what?" Caleb asked.

"I don't know, anything. We're missing our friend and need to check on her? We tracked her location to here?"

After beating on the door some more, and still no response, I walked over to one of the front windows to see if I could see anybody inside. The first window I came to the blinds were completely shut. I walked over to the second window, the blinds here were tilted slightly down but not enough to be able to see anything of value inside. Frustrated, I turned back to the front door.

"Anything?" Justine asked.

"Nope, blinds are closed," I answered.

"Caleb, do you remember the guy's name that lives here? What if he moved out after school was done for the summer? He might not even be here anymore," Justine stated.

"Honestly, I really don't know him. I'd seen him around our studio space a little bit and that one class. I only recognized him because our departments are kind of small in comparison to the other departments," Caleb replied.

"Well, this isn't getting us anywhere. We need to get inside somehow." I was frustrated, beyond frustrated and starting to get more worried.

"Wait, I hear something. Maybe someone is finally coming," Justine said moving closer to the door.

Stepping closer to the front door, I thought I heard the latch click. Maybe we were in luck. The door was flung open, and Natasha came flying out, not even bothering to shut the door behind her. She paused, startled, as she had about run the three of us over in her flight from the house. I didn't even have a chance to say a word before she was in my arms, sobbing.

"Troy! I was so scared! Please, get me the hell out of here."

"What happened? How'd you get here?" Justine asked.

"I don't really know. Please, let's just go," Natasha sobbed.

"Do you want me to go in there?" Caleb asked.

"No! Please, let's just go," Natasha cried.

"We'll figure the rest out later. Let's get her out of here." I wrapped Natasha tighter in my arms and started moving her toward Justine's car. "Here, give me your bag." Natasha slid it off her shoulder and handed it over to me.

Caleb reached over and took it from my hand. "I've got it, that way your hands are free."

"Thank you." I continued to move Natasha toward Justine's car and helped her in the backseat. I slid in next to her while Caleb got into the front with Justine.

I pulled Natasha as tightly to my side as her seatbelt would allow. Her head rested on my shoulder, her body shaking. Lightly, I brushed strands of her hair behind her ear. "Shh...you're safe now. It's going to be okay," I whispered to her. I could feel her still trembling under my touch.

Justine started the car and pulled away from the curb, her worried eyes caught mine in the rear-view mirror. I simply shrugged. I had no words. All I knew is we had found her, but what we didn't know yet is if anything else had happened to her.

"Should we go back to the dorm?" Justine asked.

A HEALING TOUCH

Caleb turned to look back at us in the backseat waiting for a response. Natasha shook her head no, mumbling so softly I could barely hear her.

"We can go to my house, it will be quieter, without everyone around on campus."

"Okay, I just need directions." Justine replied, her gaze shifting from the rear-view mirror to the road ahead.

~ *Natasha* ~

Pushing myself tighter against Troy, I tried to slow down my breathing. I was out of that hell and I was safe now. I had never expected that Troy would be at the front door, but the relief over finding him there with Justine and Caleb had been overwhelming.

How had they known I was there? And how did Caleb end up with them? So many questions, but I couldn't put the words together right now.

I was suddenly so exhausted. Every bit of energy I had left, draining from my body. Closing my eyes, I was vaguely aware of Caleb and Justine's voices from the front of the car. The steady beating of Troy's heart under my cheek was a soothing balm to the beating of my frantic one.

The slamming of a door shut startled me awake. I hadn't even realized that I'd dozed off.

"Natasha, let's get you inside." Troy helped me sit upright and unbuckle my seatbelt.

"Where are we?" I asked, somewhat disorientated.

"My house," he answered.

Troy opened the door, and reached down to help me out. He pulled me against his side as we walked together up the sidewalk to his front door, where Justine and Caleb were waiting for us. Troy released me as Justine grabbed me hugging me tightly.

"You gave us a scare," Justine whispered into my ear.

"I can't believe you guys found me. I was so scared."

Sadie came bounding out the front door barking excitingly and licked my hand in greeting. She then immediately turned, and ran back in the house.

"Well, I guess she was excited to see you?" Justine laughed.

"Her name is Sadie," I answered.

"She's quite energetic." Justine observed as she followed me into the living room while Sadie spun circles around us.

Kicking my shoes off, I pulled my legs under me as I sat on the couch. Sadie jumped up next to me and promptly laid her head in my lap. Justine sat on the other side of Sadie, while Caleb sat in a chair and Troy settled in on the other side of me. Looking between each of them I didn't even know where to start. I knew they were anxious to find out what had happened.

Looking sideways at Troy, I slipped my hand into his and I asked the question that was utmost on my mind. "How did you know I was there?"

"Justine figured it out," Troy answered.

"How?" I asked, glancing back at Justine.

"Your phone. Remember when we added that tracking app to our phones?"

"Oh, yeah. I actually had forgotten we did that, but boy am I glad we did. How did you know to track me?"

"You hadn't responded to my texts, and I ran into Justine at your room. You weren't there and she hadn't heard from you either."

"Caleb, how'd you get involved?"

"I was still in the studio. Troy had texted asking if you were still working there. When I told him no, he filled me in on how they'd tracked your phone to that house. There had been a party there right before summer and I had known one of the guys that rented a room there."

"It wasn't Gage, was it?" I asked.

"Yeah, I think that's what his name was," Caleb answered me.

"How'd you end up in that house?" Troy asked me.

"Honestly, I don't know. I was about ready to leave the studio, but then I started feeling nauseous and decided I just needed to pack up. I was walking back to the dorm and then the next thing I knew I was in that bedroom again. I have no idea how I got there."

"Wait, what do you mean 'that bedroom again,'" Justine asked.

"Exactly what I said. It was the same room."

"Did anything happen?" Justine slid closer, her voice almost a whisper.

"I don't think so. How long was I missing before you guys found me?"

"Wait, I'm lost here. What am I missing? What was the same room?" Caleb asked.

Both Justine and Troy glanced back to me, neither of them sure how to answer that question. I didn't even know how to answer it. I wasn't sure I could say the words again, to relive that horrible night again. Much less that it would mean one more person would know what had happened to me. The room was silent. I knew neither Justine or Troy would say anything. I petted the top of Sadie's head while Troy squeezed my other hand, anchoring me, giving me the courage and support in whatever I decided to do.

Pulling my gaze from Sadie, who was sleeping now practically in my lap, all attention was directed at me. Justine's gaze full of sympathy and concern, Caleb's full of confusion, and Troy's full of support and strength. Not only was I running through in my head everything that had happened to me months ago, but I was trying to make sense of the things that Gage had said after I had woken up.

After learning what had happened with Talise, I had felt a bond with her. A girl I'd never met, but one I felt that I could understand. I also knew that I didn't want to go through life feeling ashamed. I wouldn't let what had happened to me have any more control over me. There was nothing I could do to change what had happened. It couldn't be redone; but I could control what I did about it and not let it run or ruin the rest of my life.

"That night at the party, I was raped. I don't remember what happened or how I got up in that room, but I woke up the next morning there. The last thing I remembered before waking up was sitting on the front steps with you Caleb."

"You thought it was me?" Caleb whispered. "Those questions you asked after that party. You didn't know who it was, and you thought it was me?"

"I didn't know Caleb. Deep down I didn't think it was you. But I didn't know what had happened, and my last memory had been with you. I didn't know what to think."

"If you didn't know what happened, how do you know you were raped?"

"When I got back to the dorm Justine convinced me to go to the ER, they did a rape kit."

"Oh. Natasha, I'm so sorry. I had no idea, but now I can understand why you were different around me after that night," Caleb replied.

"And then when I read Talise's journal and what happened with her. I really didn't know what to think. After I saw your reaction to her journal though, I knew you weren't the one."

"So many things are starting to make more sense now," Caleb sighed.

"Okay, now that Caleb's caught up on what happened previously. What happened tonight?" Justine asked.

"Well, I woke up in that room and at first, I thought I was back in our dorm. But then I realized I wasn't, and I wasn't alone. Gage had been sitting in the corner watching me."

"Gage? He was in the room with you? Did you know him before?" Troy asked.

"No, I mean he had seemed kind of familiar, but I didn't know his name and didn't really recognize him. What was weird though, was when I first saw him in the dark shadows, he almost looked like you Caleb."

"Me? He doesn't look like me."

"Not in the light. Once he was out of the shadow, I knew it wasn't you. But when I was still groggy and the light was dim, honestly, he did resemble you. It was weird. Almost like de-ja-vu."

"Then what happened?" Troy prompted.

"I was trying not to panic, but he started talking about how I was special and chosen. I'm pretty sure he's the one that raped me that night."

"What?!?" Troy and Justine said almost in unison.

"Yeah. He didn't come out and say it directly, but it was indirectly. He explained that there was a 'special' water bottle. I was the one that took that water bottle, and that was how I was chosen."

"He spiked a water bottle?" Justine asked.

"I guess. I mean he didn't say he spiked it, just that it was special. But I'm sure that's what had happened. It's the only explanation for me getting nauseous after drinking from it. I didn't have anything else in that house. It was only the water bottle because I thought it was safe."

"What else did he tell you?" Troy asked.

I paused, remembering the rest of what he had said. "That I was special, that he was my first, and that fate had brought us together."

"He said that? He actually said that to you?" Troy said, his voice elevated and tight with anger.

"At that point, I could hear the doorbell ring and the knocking downstairs. But he didn't care. He said that whoever it was would go away. I was scared, but also angry. Realizing that he was probably the one that had raped me was just another reason I just wanted out of there so badly. When he got close enough to me, I kneed him in the groin as hard as I could, and I ran from the room. I caught site of my bag under a side table as I was reaching the front door and grabbed that too and then there you all were right at the door when I opened it."

"We need to call the police and get a report done. Do you think he was the one that wrote the notes?" Justine asked.

"Notes? What else am I missing?" Caleb questioned.

"I received a couple of strange, kind of scary notes at my desk in the studio," I replied.

"No wonder you were so jumpy in the studio lately. This is all starting to make a lot more sense now," Caleb stated.

"I didn't know who it was, and it was more frighting knowing that I was being watched. Some of the things in the notes were really creepy."

"At a minimum, you're going to need to get a restraining order. You'll also need to file a report with campus security," Troy added.

"But how did you black out tonight? You were fine earlier in the studio when I stopped by. What happened after that?" Caleb asked.

"I don't know. I was about ready to leave the studio anyway. I'd had some water from my water bottle and then I started feeling not quite right. I figured it was because I hadn't eaten since morning. I realized I was out of snacks in my bag, so I packed everything up and started walking toward the dorm. At first, I thought I was feeling better in the cool air but then the nausea got worse and that's the last thing I remember." I paused trying to grasp the last memory that I had before waking in that room. A nagging memory beyond my grasp. "Wait, I think I remember someone catching me when I fell. But I'm not exactly sure where I was on the sidewalk."

"I found your water bottle on the ground, about half way between the studio building and your dorm," Caleb added.

"I dropped it? It wasn't in my bag?"

"I came across it when I was on my way to meet Troy in the parking lot. It's still in Justine's car."

Troy pulled me tightly to his side. His arm wrapped around my shoulders. "If Gage did put something in your water bottle, there might be evidence in there. We need to turn it over."

"There's also cameras all over campus. I wonder if one of them picked up anything. You should also go talk to campus security," Caleb added.

"Are you up for that right now, Natasha? The sooner we talk to someone, the better the chances of them finding anything," Justine replied.

"Yeah. Let's go. I'm done being afraid of the shadows."

I didn't care how late it was or how exhausted I was. I was fighting back. I knew I'd forever be altered from these last few months. While I mourned what I had lost, I had also found strength and determination.

Life is always full of bumps and dead end roads. It's how you decide to navigate them, that defines you. I was also very lucky to have stumbled on some pretty amazing people that helped me along my journey.

EPILOGUE

~ *Natasha* ~

Only a couple of weeks had passed since my escape from Gage's bedroom. It had felt like a lifetime. I was currently on winter break. In the morning I was flying home to Riverview to spend Christmas and New Years with my family, as well as my best friends Bailey and Mia. Troy was even coming with me to meet my family. I was looking forward to showing him around where I had grown up. It would be a nice change of pace for a few weeks.

After we'd visited campus security, they had been able to locate the video of my collapse and being picked up and carried to the adjacent parking lot. They'd even been lucky and had been able to obtain a side profile that matched Gage. From there the police had gotten involved. I'd had to give my statements, and turn over the notes I'd received. I was so glad I hadn't thrown them away, even though I'd really wanted to when I received them. Because I'd kept them they were added to the evidence that was piling up against Gage.

The police had been granted a search warrant of the house where Gage lived and specifically Gage's room. One of the detectives working on the case had called this morning and wanted me to come down to the police station. They had located a box of additional evidence they wanted me to look through and see if I recognized anything. Troy was on his way to pick me up and was going with me.

Troy's text came through letting me know he was pulling into the parking lot. Tossing the last of my clothes into my suitcase for tomorrow's flight, I grabbed my jacket and purse and locked the door behind me.

I heard Troy's corvette before I saw it turn the corner. He pulled up to the sidewalk next to me. Doors unlocking as I reached for the door handle. I slid into the warm cabin smiling at the guy that had slowly stolen my heart over the past few months.

Troy leaned over giving me a lingering kiss, until honking behind us broke it.

"I guess someone's in a hurry." He laughed. "Are you okay?"

"Yeah. I'm ready for all this to be over though." I said as my hand interlocked with his. "Ready to go home to Riverview for a bit too. Are you ready to meet my family?" I smiled at him.

"I am. It should be fun. It's been a long time since I've visited Southern California."

We were sitting in a small, plain conference room at the police station. The chair I had sat in squeaked each time I shifted in my seat. My foot was tapping quickly under the table until Troy's hand rested on my knee, calming my nervous twitch.

Finally, Detective Bassett, who was the lead detective handling my case, entered the room. The door closing behind him as he entered. I recognized him from my previous visit to the station.

"Thank you for coming down here, Natasha. As I mentioned over the phone. We found a box in Gage's room containing some items we wanted you to look through."

"Okay."

Detective Bassett then opened a plain brown box full of sealed plastic bags. He laid each of them out on the table. Every one of them contained different pieces of jewelry or accessories. Earrings, bracelets, necklaces, hair clips. There were probably at least a dozen little bags on the table in front of me.

"What are these?" I asked as I picked up the first one, a necklace, to look at it closer.

"We think these are trophies Gage took from victims."

"You mean I wasn't the only one he did this to?"

"No, we're pretty sure he's been drugging and raping others. We just don't know how many there were or how long it had been going on. We found some files on his computer we're still going through. It looks like he had a folder of photos that he'd deleted. We're working on reconstructing the files, but have no idea if they are relevant or not. But these, we found hidden in his closet."

I carefully handled each plastic baggy, my heart breaking, wondering how many others he'd attacked. What if some of them never even knew what had happened to them? How many lives had he destroyed and for what? Was it all just some sick game to him?

My hands froze as I held a baggy with a single earring in it. The matching simple silver hoop earring was sitting in my jewelry box. I'd almost forgotten about that missing earring. I'd tossed it and the necklace I'd worn that fateful night at the bottom of my jewelry box and hadn't touched them since.

"Do you recognize that earring?" Detective Bassett asked.

"Yeah. It's mine. I have the matching one in my dorm room, with the matching necklace."

"Do you mind bringing those in for us to compare?"

"Yes, I can do that. I'm leaving for a few weeks to go home for the holidays, but I can bring them in when I return if that's okay?"

"That will be fine. And thank you for taking the time to come down here."

"What's happening with Gage?" I asked.

"He's out on bail right now. But you have your restraining order in place. Make sure you always keep that on you. If he gets near you at all, you need to call 911."

"I understand."

Troy had sat silent next to me the entire time, his hand on my knee, grounding me. But he reached for one of the baggies containing a charm bracelet. I watched as his face visibly drained of color. He turned it over in his hand, looking at each charm closer.

"Troy, what is it?" I asked.

"This was in Gage's box too?" Troy asked, his voice rough.

"Yes, why? Do you recognize it?" Detective Bassett asked.

"It was my sister's. Talise got this from my grandparents when she was sixteen. She got new charms for special events or things that were important to her. My parents got her the graduation tassel, it was the last charm she received. I'm pretty sure she was wearing it for graduation and the graduation party she went to. I'd actually forgotten about it until I saw it right now."

"Can we talk with your sister?" Detective Bassett asked.

"No, she died a little over three years ago. But we recently found some lost journal pages that she wrote about an incident that had happened at her high school graduation party. She had thought her boyfriend had raped her. After we found the pages, we confronted him he was as shocked as we were. After talking with him we were pretty sure it wasn't him. She never said anything to anyone."

"We'll need to see those pages and information on what high school she went to and where the party was. If your sister's boyfriend is available, it would be good to talk to him as well if he was at that party. Since Gage had possession of her charm bracelet, it's very likely that your sister was one of his victims too. With her passing, unless we find some other solid evidence, we'll likely not be able to prove he did anything. But this does possibly tie him to someone else. Hopefully we'll be able to find the owners of some of these other items. We will be in touch when we have more information. We'll see you both after the holidays."

"Wait, what about her clothing?" I asked, remembering the outfit that had been crumbled up in the corner.

"What clothing?"

"We found an outfit that had been tossed in the back of her closet. From what we read in her journal, it likely was the outfit she wore that night at the party," Troy explained.

"We can run it for trace evidence. We won't know unless we try it. But if it does come back with something, that would help strengthen our case. Especially to tie your sister in as a victim."

"If it's okay with your family. I'll stop by your house and pick it up this afternoon. It would be best not to have anyone else handle it."

"Yes, I know that will be fine. I'll let my parents know you'll be coming by."

Troy and I stood up and followed Detective Bassett out of the conference room door. I slid my hand into Troy's as we walked down the noisy hallway and through the lobby to the front doors.

Dark clouds threatened rain, but there were rays of light piercing through the clouds. The weather obviously couldn't make up its mind if it was going to be sunny or rainy. Cold wind whipped through my coat as we walked down the steps of the police station. Winter had arrived.

My mind raced. Could Gage have been the one that Talise had written about in her journal? I didn't even know if Gage had been living in town at the time that Talise was raped. But his possession of her charm bracelet was pretty damming. I tightened my grip on Troy's hand as we walked through the parking lot to his car. I knew he was still processing what had just happened as well.

We reached his corvette in silence. Troy walked me to the passenger door, but before he opened the door, he turned me to face him. His hand brushed along the side of my face. I looked up into his eyes that appeared green today rather than gray.

"Are you okay?" he asked as his hand slid down my side to settle at my waist.

"Actually, I am. Are you okay? I'm pretty sure you had more of a shock today than I did."

"I wish Talise was still here. I wish that she knew that it wasn't Caleb's fault. I wish you could have met her. But I'm also so thankful that you dropped into my life. If you hadn't, we might not have ever found Talise's pages. We may never have known what had happened. While it doesn't make it easier, for the first time, I feel like there's some closure. I'd like to think that Talise's death was an accident, more than intentional. I know we'll never know for sure. But for me, it's easier to accept."

My arms slipped around his waist. My hands sliding up his strong back. It was hard to believe that only months ago I feared I'd never be comfortable with a guy touching me. I had wondered if I'd ever feel normal again. With every word, encouragement, and touch Troy had broken apart all my fears. I felt at home and comfortable when I was in his arms.

But it wasn't just Troy's presence and support that got me through. I knew that what had happened to me wasn't going to control me. That was a decision I made. I wouldn't let it have that power over me, and I was the only one that could make that decision. No one else could do that for me.

Troy leaned down, his lips claiming mine. His left hand tightened on my waist, while his right hand slid behind my ear, holding my head. The kiss deepened and I felt myself melting into him. When he broke the kiss, he pulled back just slightly. His eyes searching mine.

"I love you, Natasha. Your strength, your courage, your determination, your fight. You truly are an inspiration."

Without hesitation, I also knew that with my whole heart I loved him too. I'd actually known it for awhile, but hadn't quite been able to say the words to him.

My arms slid up his back, holding him tightly against me. "I love you too, Troy. For understanding me, for supporting me, for giving me the space and encouragement that I didn't know I needed. For helping me get *me* back. I know I'm a different version of me than I was six months ago, but I finally feel like I'm more myself again."

Troy had been a gift, an unexpected gift, that I'd never expected. He had slowly crept into my world and my heart. Chipping away at the walls that I'd slammed up around myself. My attempt to protect what was left, after my world had been shattered. He helped ground me, when every inch of my body wanted to run. To help face my fear straight on. To hold my ground and not let the darkness win.

I reclaimed his lips in a kiss I never wanted to end.

A HEALING TOUCH

Acknowledgements:

Teighlor Polendo, Breanna Blackey, Jennifer Blackey, and Christina Herrara, as my beta readers.

Teighlor, who has been giving me input and advice since the very first chapter of "A Healing Heart" was spun. She was instrumental in finding some of the holes in the story.

Breanna, another set of eyes to keep me on my toes. Brea was a tremendous help during the editing of "A Healing Spirit" and graciously agreed to help once again.

Jennifer, one of my oldest childhood friends. One that I've always shared a special love of reading with since we were in junior high school. We've shared so many stories over the years. I'll never be able to read as fast as she can though!

Christina, who I connected with years ago through the book community. As she grew into her own writing and now offers author services which came at just the right time.

Sarah Bonilla Ori, to help give context to the trauma side of the topics in this book. I'm very appreciative of her willingness to take the time to provide feedback on the more clinical side of the story.

Resources:

According to www.rainn.org -

Sexual violence on college campuses is pervasive.
- 13% of all students experience rape or sexual assault through physical force, violence, or incapacitation (among all graduate and undergraduate students).
- 5.8% of students have experienced stalking since entering college.

College-age victims of sexual violence often do not report to law enforcement. - Only 20% of female student victims, age 18-24 report to law enforcement.

Sexual Assault Lifeline
If you or someone you know has experienced sexual assault.
Help is available 24/7 - visit www.rainn.org or
call 800-656-HOPE (4673)

Suicide & Crisis Lifeline
If you or someone you know is in crisis, call or text:
9-8-8 (24/7, free & confidential)

Peer to Peer support for Teens: (Teen hotline)
800-852-8336
6 pm - 10 pm PST

Suicide & Crisis Help Websites:
https://didihirsch.org/
https://afsp.org

About the Author:

MELISSA A HANSON lives in Southern California with her husband and two sons. Growing up in Southern California, inspiration for the city of "Riverview" is based on her hometown, Redlands.

Melissa's journey to writing began with a passion in reading that started in sixth grade. In high school she started writing, but writing took a back seat when she decided to pursue a career in architecture. Almost twenty years later, her first novel was written.

A Healing Heart was her first completed novel, and is book 1 of the Riverview Series. It is Bailey and Collin's story.

A Healing Spirit, is book 2 of the Riverview Series. It is Mia and Dylan's story.

A Healing Touch book 3 of the Riverview Series. It is Natasha and Troy's story.

Each book is a stand-alone novel.

While Melissa spends most days designing buildings, she still loves reading and creating stories.

Facebook: www.facebook.com/mahwriting
Instagram: www.instagram/melissa_a_hanson
Web: www.mahwriting.com

Melissa A. Hanson

Book 1—Bailey & Collin's Story

Riverview Series Book 1

Book 2—Mia & Dylan's Story

Riverview Series Book 2

Book 3—Natasha & Troy's Story

Riverview Series Book 3

284

A HEALING TOUCH

Milton Keynes UK
Ingram Content Group UK Ltd.
UKHW020627080324
438959UK00015B/685